THE BRONX COOKBOOK

The Bronx County Historical Society

THE BRONX COOKBOOK

For information address:

The Bronx County Historical Society
3309 Bainbridge Avenue
The Bronx, New York 10467

(718) 881-8900

All Photos are from
The Bronx County Historical Society Research Library

ISBN 0-941980-37-5

Cover Art - Doug Lazarus
Book Layout: Dan Eisenstein

Model kitchen in the new Parkchester housing development, 1938. This type of kitchen was typical of Bronx apartments built from the late 1930s through the 1960s. A gas range is to the right, a double sink is in the center and a refrigerator is to the left.

"Cedar Jack's" Last Stand Clam Bar in Melrose received a large patronage in the 1890s. The proprietor, the man standing at the left, offered a clam bake, clam chowder and cigars. An advertisement in his establishment promoted "Eagle Punch," an elixir good for indigestion and dyspepsia.

Bronx Cuisine? Is There Such a Thing?

The word "cuisine" comes from the French language, where it means both "kitchen" and "cooking." In America it has come to mean "style of cooking," and is generally applied to the food prepared by various cultures such as the Italians, who work wonders with pasta, the Chinese who can invent the most tasty dishes from almost any ingredient, as well as the distinctive style of French chefs, with their savory sauces. These can certainly be found in The Bronx, yet Bronx cuisine is not so easily categorized because it cannot be defined by the stereotypical fare associated with any particular cultural group. It surely is not just a hot dog at Yankee Stadium, however great that might taste. No, those are all narrow definitions. Bronx cuisine is all of that, and more!

Indeed, long before 1639, when Jonas Bronck set foot on the shores of the land we now call The Bronx, Native Americans prepared food in ways that were handed down from generation to generation, and then shared them with the diverse groups of people who came later from far off lands. Since then, each new group has been enriching the stock of tasty dishes served in the area called The Bronx. Bronck was born in Sweden and traveled extensively, while his servants were born and raised in Germany, the Netherlands, and Denmark. There can be no doubt that they prepared their meat and vegetables and baked their bread in the same manner, and style, as they did at home.

Later English settlers relished their boiled beef and roasts. The large numbers of Irish, fleeing famine in their homeland in the nineteenth century, could really enjoy the bounty of The Bronx as they seasoned their beef stew. Germans arriving in mid-century surely enjoyed the familiar aroma of sauerbraten, while Italians coming at the century's end dined on prosciutto or scampi. As each group came to live and work in The Bronx, they brought their own ethnic style of cooking, but often they became identified with one dish. The aroma of gefilte fish or latkes filled Jewish neighborhoods in the middle of the twentieth century. By century's end, African-Americans brought with them a taste for collard greens; Puerto Ricans, rice and beans; Mexicans, tacos and tamales; and the Koreans brought numerous varieties of kimchi.

Of course each group could not live on one dish alone. They contributed many dishes and variations to the rich mixture that could be called Bronx cuisine. Some opened restaurants specializing in their native cooking, sharing it with their Bronx neighbors, who learned of their delights. What, then, is Bronx cuisine?

Bronx cuisine is a gastronomical mix, a bountiful Bronx banquet. It is not uncommon to find a Bronx Jewish family serving Italian spaghetti with sweet and sour meatballs, or a Bronx Italian family enjoying potato latkes. Those from German extraction may enjoy Spanish paella, while African-American families can savor corned beef and cabbage. You surely don't have to be Jamaican to enjoy Jamaican curried goat. The Irish can appreciate Chinese shrimp Cantonese, as much as Puerto Ricans having cheesecake with their coffee.

Bronx cuisine is multifaceted. While the dishes may, at times, appear to be simple cooking, in reality, a Bronx meal can be highly cosmopolitan. The food and its preparation are drawn from a variety of cultures from all over the world.

The creative ideas and combinations of ingredients make it nearly impossible to fit some dishes into a specific category, and those with clever or odd recipe names hardly convey the content, so be sure to read the whole book. The variety of dishes Bronxites developed over the centuries is so vast, it would be impossible to present them all. What is revealed here is a taste of The Bronx, a mere sample of some favorites. "Mangia," "Enjoy," "Ess, Ess," "Come, Come."

The Editors

ACKNOWLEDGEMENTS

In a small way, this cookbook disproves the proverb that "too many cooks spoil the broth." It required the help of a small army of people. To the many cooks who took the time to share their favorites, the Society staff who solicited, collected, typed and edited them, as well as those who, over the years, donated their wonderful photos which grace the section dividers, many thanks.

While we are delighted to showcase the creativity and originality of our contributors, we tried to make it a little easier for everyone to read the entire collection. Therefore, the editors aimed at maintaining some degree of consistency in the presentation of ingredients and procedures. Also, space limitations dictated compactness and the use of some abbreviations, which are explained on the Table of Contents pages.

Since these pages can only serve as a mere taste of the multifaceted treasure we call Bronx cuisine, we have begun working on our second volume. Once again, we solicit your recipes and look forward to your support. You may use the form in the back pages of this book. Please send them to the Society. Thank you.

The Bronx County Historical Society
Cookbook Project
3309 Bainbridge Avenue
The Bronx, New York   10467

(718) 881-8900

iii

THE BRONX COOKBOOK

Compiled and edited by:

Ivette Arroyo
Peter Derrick
Dan Eisenstein
Gary Hermalyn
Jacqueline Kutner
Kathleen Pacher
Catherine Pellicano
Allen Slatky
Laura Tosi
Lloyd Ultan

The Bronx Cookbook

TABLE OF CONTENTS

Abbreviations used in this cookbook:

C. = Cup T. = Tablespoon tsp. = teaspoon pt. = pint qt. = quart
oz. = ounce lb(s). = pound(s) pkg. = package
sm. = small med. = medium lg. = large

22621B-ca

APPETIZERS

Steamed Clams
Clam Fritters
Hot Artichoke Dip
Artichoke Frittata
Gefilte Fish
Artichoke Dip
Potato Latkes
French Fried Onion Rings
Chopped Chicken Livers
Grandma's Gefilte Fish
Boxty Cakes
Sweet & Sour Meatballs
Deviled Crabs
Guacamole
Spinach Dip
Kasha with Walnuts
Paprika Rice
Cranberry Cream Mold

Mike's Deli, known for fine foods and catering, in the Arthur Avenue Market, Summer 1987. Dave Greco (left), Bronx Borough President Fernando Ferrer (center) about to sample some of their famous cheeses offered by Mike Greco. The Arthur Avenue Market is a prime source for Italian cold cuts, meats, cheese, pasta, seafood, produce, baked goods and hand-rolled cigars.

22621B-ca

STEAMED CLAMS

Vinnie Potter

24 soft-shell clams in shell

Wash clams thoroughly. In a large pot, add 1 gallon of water and ⅔ cup of salt. Add clams and let stand ¼ hour, then rinse well, do again. Place clams in steamer pot and cover. Steam until clams open, about 5 minutes. Remove any clams that do not open. Serve with butter.

CLAM FRITTERS

Charles Vogeler Company - c.1880s

25 clams, chopped fine
1 C. milk
1 C. flour
1 tsp. salt

dash of pepper to taste
2 eggs
oil for frying

Beat the eggs lightly, add milk, salt, pepper, flour, and lastly the clams. Mix thoroughly. Heat oil in a frying pan. Drop heaping spoonfuls of batter into pan. Fry until crisp.

HOT ARTICHOKE DIP

Ray Carile

1 can artichoke hearts (cut small)
¼ C. Parmesan cheese

½ C. mayonnaise

Preheat oven to 350°. Mix all ingredients. Bake 20 minutes in ovenproof dish.

ARTICHOKE FRITTATA

Katherine Morris Allan

18 oz. marinated, drained and chopped
  artichokes
½ lb. sharp cheddar cheese, grated
1 med. onion chopped

4 lightly beaten eggs
6 saltines, crushed
dash Tabasco
salt and pepper to taste

Preheat oven to 325°. Mix all ingredients, pour into buttered, ovenproof dish, 8" square. Bake 1 hour. Cut into squares. Serve hot, or at room temperature.

GEFILTE FISH

Dorothy Abrams

approximately 5 lbs. fish combining whitefish and pike
4 med. sized carrots
3 lg. onions
2 eggs
1 glass cold water
salt, white or black pepper (to taste)

Sauce:
fish heads and bones
4 lg. onions - sliced
3 med. sized carrots - sliced

This is my mother's recipe. Ask fishstore to grind fish. Place the ground fish in a chopping bowl. Grind 4 medium sized carrots and 3 large onions and place in the chopping bowl with the ground fish. Add two eggs to the mixture and start chopping, adding water a little at a time, while continuing to chop to get a firm consistency. Taste fish and add salt and pepper to achieve a nice taste. Wash fish bones and fish heads thoroughly and place in a large pot, filling pot half way with cold water, add 4 large onions sliced and 3 medium carrots cleaned and sliced. Bring to a boil, adding salt and pepper.

While waiting for water to come to a boil you may begin to form fish balls. You may want to wet hands so you may handle fish bails easily. When water comes to a boil, begin placing the fish balls into the water. When all fish balls are in water, cover the pot and lower flame and keep to a slow boil. Continue to taste fish and add salt and pepper to taste. Replenish with additional cold water, so fish is always covered with water. Cover pot and remain on low flame for one and one-half hours. Towards end of cooking if too much water remains, remove cover and let boil a little longer so water evaporates. Let cool and when it is cold, remove each fish ball to a plate. Strain the sauce and dispose of fish heads and bones and onions, keeping sliced carrots to garnish fish. Refrigerate the fish and sauce. You may place sliced carrots either on fish balls or in the sauce.

ARTICHOKE DIP

Ronnie Greenberg

1 can artichokes (in water),
   drained and chopped
1 C. mayonnaise
1 C. Parmesan cheese

breadcrumbs
pepper
garlic powder

Mix artichokes, mayonnaise and Parmesan cheese in a baking pan. Sprinkle top with breadcrumbs, pepper and garlic powder. Bake ½ hour at 350°. Keep warm and serve with Tortilla chips.

POTATO LATKES

Barbara Levine

3 C. grated potatoes
½ C. shredded onion
2 beaten eggs
2 T. white flour

1 tsp. salt
2 to 3 T. rendered chicken fat or
    vegetable cooking oil
dairy sour cream or applesauce

Stir together potatoes, onion, eggs, flour, and salt in bowl. Mix well. Grease a skillet with melted chicken fat or vegetable oil. Drop batter by tablespoonfuls onto skillet. Spread the batter slightly. Fry till browned, 2 minutes per side. Serve hot with sour cream or applesauce. Serves 6 to 8.

FRENCH FRIED ONION RINGS

Donald Duncan

4 lg. onions, 2 - 3 lbs.
1 C. milk
1 C. water

1 C. breadcrumbs
2 egg whites
oil for frying

Cut skinned onion into ¼" slices. Soak onions in liquid (milk and water) and then in a batter of breadcrumbs and egg whites. Cover rings with batter and fry in a skillet until light brown.

CHOPPED CHICKEN LIVERS

Mrs. Berg

I lb. chicken livers
¼ C. finely chopped onion
¼ C. rendered chicken fat
3 finely chopped hard-boiled eggs

1 tsp. salt, ¼ tsp. pepper
1 lb. lettuce leaf
assorted crackers

Cut large chicken livers in half. In a skillet, combine chicken livers, onion, and chicken fat. Cook, covered, over medium heat till onion is tender but not brown, about 10 minutes. Cool.

Remove livers (reserve onion and any pan juices); chop fine. Combine 2 eggs with chopped livers, onion, pan juices, salt, and ¼ tsp. pepper. Cover and chill 3 hours or overnight.

To serve, place a mound of mixture on lettuce. Use remaining egg yolk and egg white as garnish. Serve with crackers.

GRANDMA'S GEFILTE FISH

Helene Wayne

3 lbs. sliced onions	salt, pepper, sugar
3 onions, diced	3 eggs
4 carrots sliced	water
2 carrots to chop	matzo meal
fish bones	horseradish

fish - pike, winter carp, whitefish - approx. 5 lbs. in total.
   Have fishstore bone all fish and save the large bones.

1. Place sliced onions in large pot of salted water. Bring to boil.
2. Dice 3 onions. Prepare 4 sliced carrots, set aside.
3. Place fish bones in the salted water and let cook to boil.
4. Chop together fish, 3 diced onions and 2 carrots.
5. Add salt, pepper, sugar, 3 eggs, a little water, mix, thicken with matzo meal.
6. Make patties, drop into boiling water. Simmer 1½ hours. Add the 4 sliced carrots   and let simmer for another hour.

Refrigerate, serve with horseradish.

BOXTY CAKES

Kay Gleeson

½ lb. hot cooked potatoes	1 to 1½ C. buttermilk
½ lb. grated raw potatoes	salt and pepper
2 C. flour	butter for frying
1 tsp. baking soda	

Drain, peel, and mash hot potatoes. Stir in grated raw potatoes, flour, and baking soda. Add salt and pepper to taste. Mix well with enough buttermilk to make a stiff batter. Shape into 3" patties about ¼" thick and fry on a greased griddle until crispy and golden on both sides. Makes 12 cakes.

SWEET & SOUR MEATBALLS

Robert Black

2 lbs. ground beef
⅔ C. matzo meal
2 eggs slightly beaten
½ minced onion
1 tsp. salt
¼ tsp. pepper

1 lg. onion diced
1 C. brown sugar
sour salt (citric acid) to taste
1 (11 oz.) can tomato sauce
½ C. water

Combine beef, matzo meal, eggs, minced onion, salt, pepper. Shape into meatballs. In a large pot, combine diced onion, sugar, sour salt, tomato sauce and water. Add meatballs. Bring to a boil, reduce heat and simmer for 1 hour. Add sugar or sour salt to your taste. Serves 6.

DEVILED CRABS

Charles Vogeler Company - c.1880s

several boiled crabs
breadcrumbs - 1 T. for every five
spoonfuls of meat juice of one lemon
pinch of grated lemon peel

¼ tsp. mustard
pinch of cayenne pepper
¼ tsp. salt
2 T. butter

Boil the crabs. Let crabs cool, then pick meat from the shells and cut fine. Mix crab meat with lemon juice, grated lemon peel, mustard, cayenne pepper and salt. Melt the butter in a saucepan, add the crab mixture and toss about with a fork until very hot. Fill the back shells of the crabs with this, stick tiny bits of butter on top, sift breadcrumbs over all. Cook to a light brown in the oven. Serve hot. Pass lemons and crackers with this dish.

GUACAMOLE

Steve Schwartz

3 ripe avocadoes
1 tomato
1 scallion
1 T. fresh lemon juice

½ tsp. garlic powder
salt
OPTIONAL: hot pepper, to taste

Chop scallion and tomato. Scoop out avocadoes, and mash up with a fork. Add garlic powder, tomato, scallion, lemon juice, and few pinches of salt (and perhaps hot pepper, to taste). Mix thoroughly. Serve with tortilla chips.

SPINACH DIP

Diane Steinberg

1 pt. sour cream
1 C. mayonnaise
¾ C. green onions, chopped (about 2 bunches)
¼ C. dried parsley

½ tsp. dried dill
1 tsp. salt
dash of pepper
1 pkg. frozen chopped spinach

Mix all ingredients except spinach a day before using. Refrigerate. Defrost spinach, drain thoroughly and add to the mixture.

KASHA WITH WALNUTS

Dolores Lessner

4 T. butter or margarine
½ C. chopped walnuts
2 C. med. Kasha

2 T. instant minced onion
3 C. beef broth
3 T. soy sauce

In a heavy skillet melt 1 T. butter or margarine, then saute chopped walnuts, till golden brown. Set aside in small bowl. Heat remaining 3 T. butter/margarine in skillet to saute Kasha over medium heat, stirring constantly until golden toasted. Add onion, beef broth, soy sauce. Cover tightly, simmer gently 15 minutes or until all liquids are absorbed. Stir in sauted walnuts. Serve at once.

PAPRIKA RICE

Tina Walker

1 C. long grain rice
1 T. salt
2 C. water
1 T. paprika

2 T. butter
pinch white pepper
1 T. celery salt

Wash rice well. Boil water and add salt and rice. Boil 5 minutes. Do not stir. Drain off water. Add paprika and butter. Stir with a fork until blended. Return to heat. Cover and steam for about 5 minutes. Remove cover, continue to simmer for 15 minutes longer over very low heat.

CRANBERRY CREAM MOLD

Gloria Magat

1 pkg. cherry gelatin
1 C. hot water
1 C. sour cream

1 (16 oz.) can, whole berry cranberry
    sauce, drained
OPTIONAL: ¼ C. chopped walnuts

Dissolve gelatin in hot water. Chill until cool and starting to thicken. Break up cranberry sauce with fork so there are no chunks. Stir into gelatin. Add walnuts if desired. Beat sour cream until soft and smooth, fold into mixture and mix thoroughly. Pour into lightly greased mold. Refrigerate overnight. Unmold by turning mold over platter and running hot water for 15 - 20 seconds over back of mold pan. Serves 4 to 6. This recipe can be easily doubled for more than six servings. Excellent for turkey, chicken and pot roast.

NOTES

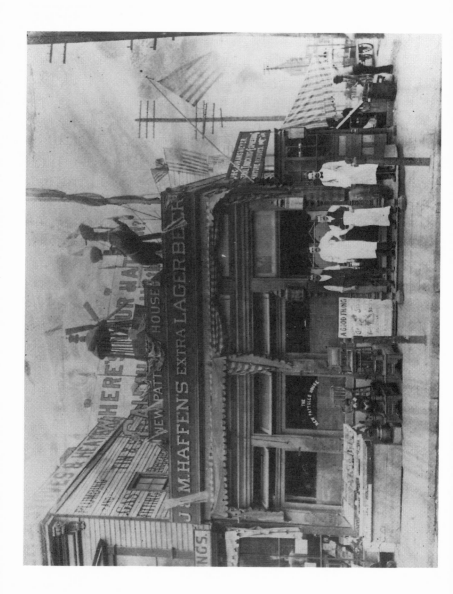

SOUPS & SANDWICHES

Fresh Carrot & Potato Soup
Chicken Soup
Sweet Potato Soup
Chicken Soup Stock
Egg Drop Soup
Lobster Chowder
Caribbean Soup (Sancocho - Vegetable Stew)
Fresh Vegetable Soup
Grilled Cheese Sandwich
Chicken Salad Sandwich
Ham and Cheese and Turkey Sandwich
Grilled Reuben
Salmon and Egg Sandwiches

FRESH CARROT & POTATO SOUP

Marco Greco

10 lg. carrots
3 lg. potatoes
salted water
2 lg. onions, minced

¼ C. olive oil
2 cloves garlic, minced
salt and pepper
2 T. dill

Clean carrots and potatoes. Leave carrots whole and cube potatoes. Put carrots and potatoes in salted boiling water (just enough to cover vegetables). When vegetables are tender, remove from water, saving the water (broth).

Saute onions in olive oil; when tender, add garlic. Puree carrots (food processor) and add to onion and garlic mixture. Add some broth to mixture, depending on thickness consistency. Add remaining ingredients, including potatoes. Simmer covered approximately 10 minutes. Garnish with fresh dill.

CHICKEN SOUP

Lena Chednofsky

1 tsp. premium olive oil
2 stalks celery, finely chopped
3 lg. carrots, sliced
3 C. chicken stock
2 C. water

pinch of salt and pepper to taste
⅓ C. fresh parsley or
    1 - 2 tsp. dried parsley
1 C. shredded chicken
½ C. frozen peas

Cook in a 4-qt. pot until moderately done: 1 tsp. of olive oil, celery, carrots. Then add: 3 cups chicken stock, 2 cups of water, pinch of salt and pepper to taste, parsley, shredded chicken, and ½ cup of frozen peas. Cook until done.

SWEET POTATO SOUP

Elizabeth Beirne

2 lg. sweet potatoes
2 lg. carrots
1 onion

1 stalk celery
1 qt. chicken stock

Peel all vegetables, keep as large pieces. Place all in chicken stock, bring to a boil. Lower heat and simmer until ingredients are cooked, 1 to 2 hours.

CHICKEN SOUP STOCK

Sarah Cohen

1 fresh 4 lb. chicken
New York City water
1 lb. chopped onion
2 lg. carrots, sliced

1 tsp. salt
pinch of pepper
1 garlic clove
⅓ C. white wine

Buy a good fresh chicken, preferably from the Arthur Avenue Poultry Market--
It's all in the chicken! Cut the chicken into small pieces and place into a large
8-qt. pot of fresh, cold, New York City water. Add one pound of cut onion, 2
large sliced carrots, a tsp. of salt, pinch of pepper, 1 garlic clove, and ⅓ cup of
white wine. Place covered pot on burner till it boils, simmer for 3 hours.

Remove bones and meat; strain the liquid into containers and refrigerate. Before
using or freezing, remove the congealed fat on top of the stock. For clearer
consomme style, strain it again through a white handkerchief or cheesecloth.

EGG DROP SOUP

Sherry Varon

1 qt. of chicken broth
1 T. cornstarch

2 beaten eggs
sliced scallions

Blend 1 quart of chicken broth and 1 T. of cornstarch. Cook and stir until
thickened. Pour in beaten eggs, stir once gently. Remove from heat. Pour into
bowls and garnish with sliced scallions.

LOBSTER CHOWDER

Charles Vogeler Company - c.1880s

meat of 1 lobster
1 qt. milk
1 tsp. salt
¼ tsp. cayenne pepper

2 T. butter rolled in 1 T. flour
pinch of club soda in the milk
6 Boston crackers, split and buttered

Scald the milk and stir in seasoning, butter and flour. Cook 1 minute, add the
lobster and simmer 5 minutes. Line a tureen with the toasted and buttered
crackers, dipping each quickly in boiling water before putting it in place, and
pour in the chowder. Send around sliced lemon with it.

CARIBBEAN SOUP (SANCOCHO - VEGETABLE STEW)

Manuel Rodriguez

A:
12 C. water
1 T. salt
1 onion, peeled
2 tomatoes
1 green pepper
1 sweet chili pepper
3 fresh cilantro leaves
2 fresh corn kernels, halved
1 T. salt
B:
1 lb. lean beef
½ lb. lean pork meat with bone

C:
½ lb. white yautia
½ lb. yellow yautia
½ small pumpkin
½ lb. potatoes
½ lb. ñame
½ lb. sweet potatoes
D:
1 lg. green plantain, peeled & diced
1 lg. ripe plantain, peeled & diced
½ C. tomato sauce

1. In large kettle (about 12 qts.) mix ingredients in A, bring rapidly to a boil.
2. Clean and wash meats, cut into 1" cubes, add to kettle; cover and   reduce heat to moderate, about an hour.
3. Wash vegetables in C, cut in pieces; add to kettle.
4. Rinse green plantain in salted water. Drain, add to kettle together with ripe plantain.
5. Add tomato sauce and bring rapidly to a boil; cover and cook over moderate heat until tender. Serve hot.

FRESH VEGETABLE SOUP

G. Hermalyn

Only use fresh vegetables:
1 lg. green pepper
2 onions
2 garlic cloves
2 white potatoes
2 lg. sweet potatoes
4 carrots
3 celery stalks

2 T. premium olive oil
3 C. chicken stock
3 C. water
1 tsp. dried basil
¼ tsp. salt, ¼ tsp. pepper (to taste)
½ C. frozen peas
*OPTIONAL: ½ cup angel hair noodles

Cut up vegetables. Heat up 2 T. of premium olive oil in 4-quart soup pot. Add green pepper, onions. garlic, potatoes, sweet potatoes, carrots and celery. Saute gently for 10 minutes or so. Then add chicken stock, water, basil, salt and pepper and frozen peas. Cover pot, simmer for about 90 minutes. Stir occasionally. *Add ½ C. uncooked angel hair noodles, simmer 30 more minutes.

GRILLED CHEESE SANDWICH

Joy Musto

cheese (your choice)
hot mustard
French bread

Between 2 thick slices of French bread, add hot mustard and your choice of cheese. Spread butter on top and bottom slices. Grill on both sides until cheese has melted.

CHICKEN SALAD SANDWICH

Gerritt Smith

1 C. finely chopped cooked chicken
⅓ C. mayonnaise
dash of lemon juice

dash of salt and pepper to taste
parsley
⅛ C. chopped almonds

Mix all ingredients, chill, and spread on bread. Try pumpernickel!

HAM AND CHEESE AND TURKEY SANDWICH

Charles Lobl

1 - 12" loaf Italian bread
sliced ham and turkey
sliced Swiss or American cheese
mustard or mayonnaise

lettuce and tomato
Optional: onion slices, olives and/or dill
pickles

Split loaf lengthwise, scoop out some of the center. Add a smear of Goulden's or deli mustard, or mayonnaise, according to your taste. Add slices of boiled ham and turkey, Swiss or American cheese, lettuce, tomato, and perhaps onion slices, olives, or dill pickles.

GRILLED REUBEN

Joy Musto

2 slices pumpernickel or rye bread
Thousand Island dressing
1 thick slice of Swiss or American
cheese

sauerkraut
cooked or canned corned beef
butter

Spread on 1 piece of bread the Thousand Island dressing, and add the cheese, the sauerkraut, corned beef and second slice of bread. Spread butter on top and bottom slices and grill on both sides until hot and cheese melts. Serve hot.

SALMON AND EGG SANDWICHES

Sol Montcalm Hermalyn

1 can salmon
3 hard-boiled eggs
OPTIONAL: onion slices

mayonnaise
salt and pepper to taste
toast or hard Kaiser roll with poppy
    seeds

Chop salmon and eggs in a hand chopper until fine (add onion slices, if desired). Mix with mayonnaise and salt and pepper, to taste. Serve on toast or a hard Kaiser roll with poppy-seeds.

SALADS & VEGETABLES

Mrs. Bob Hope's Antipasto Salad
Finnish Cucumber Salad (Kurkkusalaatti)
Health Salad
Shrimp Salad (Ceviche)
Goldie's Chopped Vegetable Salad
Cole Slaw
Cole Slaw (German Style Slaw)
Cran-Raspberry Salad
Roasted Pumpkin or other Winter Squash
Jerusalem Artichokes
Baked Sweet Potato
Rice and Beans (Puerto Rican Style)
Bajan Style Pigeon Peas
Curried Lentils
Baked Bean Dish
Creamed Turnips
Baked Cauliflower
Celeriac or Celery Root
Fried Cucumbers
Italian Green Beans
Green Bean Stir-Fry
Duchess Potatoes
Stewed Sweet Potatoes
Italian Fried Zucchini Flowers
Stringbeans, Potatoes and Bacon
French Fries
Deviled Tomatoes
Scalloped Squash
Indian Succotash
Stewed Tomatoes

MRS. BOB HOPE'S ANTIPASTO SALAD

Mary T. Placko

1 celery heart, sliced thin
1 can (1 lb. 4 oz.) chick peas, drained
1 jar (6 oz.) marinated artichoke hearts,
   quartered, reserve liquid
1 can (2 oz.) anchovy fillets,
   drained and cut up
1 can or jar (4 oz.) pimentos,
   drained and diced
½ lb. Italian Genoa salami,
   cut in ¼" cubes

1 pkg. (8 oz.) mozzarella cheese,
   cut in ¼" cubes
12 pitted black olives
½ head iceberg lettuce,
   cut in bite-size pieces
6 T. olive oil
5 T. wine vinegar
1 tsp. salt
¼ tsp. pepper

1. Combine chick peas, artichoke hearts, anchovies, pimentos, salami, mozzarella cheese, olives, lettuce, and celery in a large bowl.
2. Combine olive oil, vinegar, salt and pepper, and artichoke heart liquid in a jar with a tight lid; shake well to mix. Pour over vegetable mixture, toss lightly.

Makes about 3 lbs.

FINNISH CUCUMBER SALAD (KURKKUSALAATTI)

Vesa J. Nelson

1 (10 - 12") European style cucumber
   or 2 (6") cucumbers
2 T. dried dill weed or chopped fresh
dill (to taste)

½ C. white vinegar
½ C. white sugar
¼ C. cool water
1 tsp. salt

1. Cut washed unpeeled cucumbers into round paper-thin slices.
2. In a medium bowl, layer sliced cucumbers, sprinkling dill between layers.
3. In a 2-cup measure, combine vinegar, sugar, water and salt.
4. Pour over cucumber mixture.
5. Refrigerate 4 - 5 hours.
6. Serve.

Serves 4 to 6.

HEALTH SALAD

Kathleen Nanetti

1 head cabbage (about 1½ lbs.)
   finely shredded
2 med. carrots, shredded (1¼ C.)
1 med. green pepper, (1 C.),
   finely chopped
1 sm. red onion, thinly sliced (1 C.)

½ C. cider vinegar
⅓ C. sugar
¼ C. corn oil
½ tsp. celery seed
½ tsp. garlic salt

In a very large bowl, toss together cabbage, carrot, green pepper and onion. Mix together vinegar, sugar, corn oil, celery seed and garlic salt. Pour over cabbage mixture. Cover. Marinate in refrigerator overnight. Makes about 7 cups.

SHRIMP SALAD (CEVICHE)

Pedro Rodriguez

4 lbs. med. shrimp
4 lemons
2 green or red peppers
1 lg. onion

2 T. vinegar
1 oz. oil
4 oz. olives
1 tsp. Adobo (seasoning)

Peel off skin of shrimp and devein (do not cook). Cut up peppers, onion and olives in small pieces. Squeeze juice of all of the lemons into a large bowl. Now add to lemon juice: peppers, onion, vinegar, oil, olives and Adobo. Add shrimp and stir. Toss thoroughly every hour for 2 or 3 hours until shrimps are firm. Serve.

GOLDIE'S CHOPPED VEGETABLE SALAD

Lucy Greenstein

1 head of lettuce
1 bunch radishes
1 lg. red pepper
1 lg. cucumber
1 lg. carrot, grated
1 sm. jar stuffed olives
2 stalks celery

3 - 4 plum tomatoes
4 scallions
3 sprigs parsley
1 lemon
3 T. olive oil
salt and pepper

Cut up each vegetable separately and place into a large bowl; slice olives and add to bowl. (All this may be done earlier and refrigerated.) When ready to serve, add the juice of a lemon and 3 T. olive oil. Salt and pepper to taste and mix well.

COLE SLAW

Edith Duncan

1 head cabbage	½ C. boiling water
1 C. vinegar	½ C. milk or cream
1 tsp. mustard	1 T. butter
3 T. sugar	3 egg yolks
1 tsp. salt	

Shred, slice, or chop very fine desired amount of cabbage, place in salad dish.

Pour over the cabbage a sauce made thus: Bring 1 cup vinegar to a boil, add mixture of 1 tsp. mustard, 3 T. of sugar and 1 tsp. of salt, scalded together with ½ cup of boiling water. Add ½ cup of milk or cream and a lump of butter; let boil again, stirring constantly, and stir in the beaten yolks of 3 eggs. Pour hot over cabbage as soon as sauce is stirred to an even consistency. Let cool, place in the refrigerator and serve cold.

COLE SLAW (GERMAN STYLE SLAW)

W. K. Wucherer

1 lg. head cabbage, shredded	1 C. vinegar
1 Bermuda onion, minced	1 T. salt
1 green pepper, chopped	1 tsp. dry mustard
1 C. sugar	1 T. celery seed
¾ C. oil	

Place cabbage, onion and pepper in a large non-metal pan. In a saucepan, bring the sugar, oil, vinegar, salt, mustard and celery seed to a rolling boil. Pour over cabbage immediately, stir. Put into a large container, seal and refrigerate.

CRAN-RASPBERRY SALAD

Audrey Noonan

1 (6-oz.) pkg. raspberry gelatin (or Jello)	1 (15¼ oz.) can crushed pineapple (drained)
1½ C. boiling water	½ C. chopped walnuts
1 pt. raspberry sherbet	OPTIONAL: 1 C. dairy sour cream
1 (16 oz.) can jellied cranberry sauce	

Dissolve gelatin in boiling water. Add sherbet, stir until completely blended. Thoroughly mix cranberry sauce with pineapple, then fold with walnuts into gelatin. Turn into 9×9" pan or dish. Refrigerate until firm, cut into squares. Remove from dish, spread sour cream over top just before serving, if desired.

ROASTED PUMPKIN OR OTHER WINTER SQUASH

Anthony Signoreilli

1 pumpkin or other Winter squash
butter

Cut through middle, take out all the seeds; put halves together and roast in an oven. When done and the pulp is soft, add butter as a topping.

JERUSALEM ARTICHOKES

Bro. Edward Quinn

1 lb. washed and peeled Jerusalem
   artichokes
2 T. butter
2 T. flour

½ tsp. salt
dash of white pepper
1 C. light cream or milk
¼ C. chopped parsley

Boil artichokes until tender, 10 to 15 minutes; drain. Melt butter, blend into batter: flour, salt and pepper, and cream. Cook till it thickens and bubbles. Stir in parsley. Serve over sliced artichokes.

BAKED SWEET POTATO

Barry Telphy

4 C. shredded raw sweet potatoes
   (1 lb.)
1 C. water
½ C. packed brown sugar

½ tsp. salt
¼ tsp. ground ginger
2 T. butter

Combine potato, water, sugar, salt, and ginger in a 1-qt. casserole smeared with butter. Bake at 350° till mixture is tender and caramelized, stirring occasionally, about 2 hours.

RICE AND BEANS (PUERTO RICAN STYLE)

Rosa Delgada

1 onion, chopped
6 T. "sofrito"
4 T. oil
1 T. colored oil

1 can red beans
3 C. rice
salt to taste
water to cook rice

Saute the onions and "sofrito" in oil for several minutes. Add the beans without the liquid. Add the water; bring to a boil, add the rice. Salt to taste. Boil uncovered till dry, then cover and cook over medium heat until tender.

BAJAN STYLE PIGEON PEAS

Pearl Blanchette

1 pkg. (16 oz.) dry pigeon peas
½ C. onion, chopped
½ C. diced green pepper

1 lb. spicy sausage meat
salt and pepper
water

Inspect peas for foreign substances, then rinse. Cover with cold water and soak overnight. When ready to cook peas, drain, rinse and cover with fresh cold water. Cook approximately 1½ hours or until peas are tender and water has evaporated. Saute onions and peppers. Cook sausage and then dice or cut into thin slices. Add chopped onion, diced green pepper, and sausage to peas. Season to taste with salt and pepper. Mix well and cook over low flame for 15 minutes. Serve over rice.

CURRIED LENTILS

Leslie Ann Hogan

1 C. lentils
2½ - 3 C. water
1 bay leaf
1 - 2 tsp. salt
1 med. onion, chopped
1 clove garlic, minced
1 - 2 T. curry powder

½ tsp. turmeric
½ tsp. ground ginger
¼ tsp. cumin
¼ tsp. coriander
¼ tsp. chili powder
2 T. lemon juice
handful chopped fresh parsley

Combine lentils, 2½ cups water and spices in large pot. Bring to a boil and immediately lower heat to lowest level and simmer for about 45 - 60 minutes. Stir occasionally to avoid lentils sticking to bottom of pot. As lentils absorb water and become tender, add more water as desired. When all water is absorbed and lentils are soft, remove from heat. Add lemon juice and parsley, combine gently with entire mixture, trying not to mash lentils.

Can be served immediately, hot, with brown rice, cucumbers thinly sliced, plain yogurt, and pita bread. But - best the next day. Great to bring to a picnic or pot-luck party.

BAKED BEAN DISH

Peggy Keating

1 can B & M Baked Beans
1 can red kidney beans
1 can green lima beans
4 strips bacon, raw
1 lg. onion sliced thin

½ C. ketchup
2 T. brown sugar
2 T. vinegar
½ tsp. dry mustard

Fry bacon until crisp and remove. Cook onions in bacon fat until transparent. Mix ketchup, sugar, vinegar and mustard in with the onions. Put beans in ovenproof casserole, add above mixture, and top with cooked bacon pieces. Cover casserole and bake in 350° oven until heated and bubbly.

CREAMED TURNIPS

Charles Vogeler Company - c.1880s

1 med. turnip
1 - 2 T. butter

3 T. milk
salt and pepper

Peel the turnip and let sit in cold water for ½ hour. Cook till tender in hot salted water; drain. Place in a clean pot and beat in the butter and milk. Season with salt and pepper. The lumps should be rubbed out and the turnip should be a smooth puree.

BAKED CAULIFLOWER

Greist Family

1 whole cauliflower
1 C. melted butter

½ C. breadcrumbs
OPTIONAL: Serve with vinegar or lemon

Boil whole cauliflower until tender, but not until it breaks. Remove from pot; split down the middle with a sharp knife; lay the cut sides downward in a bake dish; pour over and about it the cup of butter, and sift the breadcrumbs on top. Set in the oven at 350° till it begins to brown.

CELERIAC OR CELERY ROOT

Greist Family

This knobby, tough root can be a most subtly flavored vegetable, eaten raw in salads, cooked in soup, or pureed with potatoes. It can be hard to peel, so cut into slices first. Try steaming for 25 minutes and serve with a white sauce or cheese sauce. To make the flavor more delicate for use in salads, blanch 1 - 2 minutes after peeling. A little lemon juice in the water will keep it white.

FRIED CUCUMBERS

Charles Vogeler Company - c.1880s

3 or 4 cucumbers
2 eggs, beaten
½ C. breadcrumbs

salt and pepper
oil for frying
OPTIONAL: lemon juice

Peel off the skin of the cucumbers and slice lengthwise into thick pieces and lay in cold water for ½ hour; wipe dry, dip in beaten egg, then in breadcrumbs that are seasoned with salt and pepper and fry in hot oil. Drain and serve while hot. You may like to squeeze some lemon on each slice.

ITALIAN GREEN BEANS

Laura Tosi

1 T. onion, minced
¼ tsp. minced garlic
1 T. water
2 T. olive oil

1 lb. green beans
1 T. basil, chopped fine
1 tsp. salt
⅛ tsp. black pepper

In a large skillet heat oil, and add the onion and garlic; saute for 5 minutes. Reduce heat and add the green beans, basil, salt, black pepper and the T. of water. Cover and simmer for approx. 5 minutes, or until beans are crisp and tender, stirring a few times. Watch carefully to prevent beans from burning. Put into a dish and serve. Serves 6 to 8.

GREEN BEAN STIR-FRY

Maralyn Alpert

4 tsp. peanut oil
1 lb. green beans with ends removed
½" ginger root, peeled and grated, or
    1 chopped garlic clove
¼ C. water

3 scallions - chopped
1 tsp. brown sugar
1 tsp. dark soy sauce
½ tsp. sesame seeds

In a wok heat the oil, add beans, ginger root (or garlic) for 1 minute. Add sugar and water. Reduce heat and cook for 5 minutes or so until the beans become tender. Stir in soy sauce, sprinkle with scallions and sesame seeds. Serves 4.

DUCHESS POTATOES

Robert Black

8 med.-sized potatoes - 2⅓ lbs.
¼ C. butter
2 beaten egg yolks

dash of dry mustard
salt and pepper to taste
1 egg

Wash potatoes well, remove sprouts and blemishes, and pare. Cook covered 20 - 40 minutes in 5 cups boiling water to which ½ tsp. salt has been added. When they are tender, drain well and allow to dry. Put them through a food mill or ricer. While still hot, add all other ingredients and mix together well. Preheat oven to 400°. Shape the potato mixture into flat cakes on a floured board. Place the cakes in a buttered baking dish. Brush with a slightly beaten egg. Bake until golden and serve at once. Serves 8.

STEWED SWEET POTATOES

Charles Vogeler Company - c.1880s

2 lbs. boiled sweet potatoes, cold
1 T. butter per C. of diced potatoes

1 C. gravy or stock
1 T. flour
salt and pepper to taste

Dice the cold, boiled potatoes. For each cupful of potatoes mix together 1 heaping T. of butter. Put mixture into frying pan, and when hot, stir and toss until slightly browned and well glazed. Have ready in a separate saucepan over flame, a cupful of got gravy or stock; season well with salt and pepper, thicken with flour and put the potatoes into it. Remove and keep warm. Let sit for 5 minutes and serve.

ITALIAN FRIED ZUCCHINI FLOWERS

Jacqueline Kutner

2 T. vegetable oil
10 fresh picked zucchini flowers
2 eggs

salt and pepper
1 C. seasoned breadcrumbs with some
white flour added in

Pick large unbruised orange zucchini flowers from plant. Wash thoroughly inside and out. Mix eggs with dash of salt and pepper; dip zucchini flowers in egg on both sides, then dip into the breadcrumbs. Fry until golden brown on both sides; blot off extra oil on paper towel. Serve hot! Sounds weird, but tastes delicious!

STRINGBEANS, POTATOES AND BACON

Geri Olbermann

2 lbs. fresh stringbeans
10 slices lean bacon, quartered
1 med. onion, chopped

5 C. water
salt and pepper to taste
3 C. sliced potatoes

Wash and trim stringbeans. Cut into 1" diagonal slices. Fry bacon until crisp. Remove and set aside. Reserve ¼ cup of bacon drippings. Saute onion in drippings until tender. Add water, bacon, beans, salt and pepper, and simmer for 15 minutes. Add potatoes and cook until potatoes are done. Serves 6.

FRENCH FRIES

Tom Gibson

8 lg. potatoes

1 C. olive oil

Slice potatoes crosswise to make the largest possible pieces and place into a skillet with the olive oil. Turn when brown. Drain oil. Salt and pepper to taste.

DEVILED TOMATOES

Charles Vogeler Company - c.1880s

4 lg. firm tomatoes
3 T. oil
3 T. vinegar
3 egg yolks, beaten lightly

1 tsp. sugar
½ tsp. mustard
½ tsp. salt
pinch of cayenne pepper

Pare large, firm tomatoes, then cut crosswise into thick slices and broil. Lay them on a hot dish. Put sugar, pepper, salt and mustard into vinegar, and heat to a boil. Beat oil drop by drop into whipped yolks. When you have a rich creamy mixture, stir the boiling vinegar into it gradually. Pour this over the tomatoes.

SCALLOPED SQUASH

Charles Vogeler Company - c.1880s

2 C. boiled squash
2 eggs
1 T. melted butter

½ C. milk
salt and pepper
½ C. breadcrumbs

Beat eggs, butter, milk, and squash together. Pour into a buttered baking dish, sift the breadcrumbs over the top, and bake covered at 350° for ½ hour and then brown lightly. Serve hot.

INDIAN SUCCOTASH

G. Hermalyn

1 C. cooked fresh lima beans   1 T. butter
1 C. cooked fresh corn   ½ tsp. salt

Combine ingredients and heat in a double-boiler for a few minutes.

STEWED TOMATOES

Mildred Nestor

several fresh large ripe tomatoes   1 onion, minced
1 clove garlic, minced   salt and pepper
1 green pepper, chopped   butter
water   OPTIONAL: celery, chopped
flour

In a large kettle, bring water to a boil. Dip a few tomatoes at a time. Remove after a minute or so and dip into cold water. Peel skins, end stems, and any bruised areas. Place into another pot and mash. Repeat until tomatoes are finished. Add minced garlic, onion and green pepper, also chopped celery if desired. Salt and pepper to taste. Cook until tender. You may wish to prepare your celery, garlic and green pepper in advance. Flour may be mixed with some butter to thicken.

TO JAR: Sterilize jars and covers in boiling water and fill with tomatoes. Seal, cool, and store in refrigerator. Can be eaten cold or served hot with a pat of butter.

BREADS & ROLLS

Bogman Bread
Passover Rolls
"Chocolate" (Carob) Rye Bread
Zucchini Quick Bread
Aunt Nora's Irish Soda Bread
Raisin Currant Bread
Bagels
Irish Soda Bread
Irish Soda Bread
Blueberry Lemon Loaf
Scones

BOGMAN BREAD

G. Hermalyn

2 C. warm water
1 T. dry yeast
2 T. honey
2 T. light oil (canola or sesame)
2 tsp. salt
1 C. whole wheat flour

4 to 5 C. unbleached white flour
4 T. raw or toasted wheat germ
1 tsp. blackstrap molasses
2 egg whites
½ C. non-fat milk

Put 2 cups warm water in a large mixing bowl, with the honey and the dry yeast, and stir, then leave alone. After yeast becomes foamy, add oil, salt, eggs, molasses, whole wheat flour. Beat well, 150 - 250 strokes. Add wheat germ, milk, and then the final cups of flour. Knead for at least 10 minutes. Let the dough rise in a warm place. To test, press your finger into the dough an inch or so, if hole remains, it is ready to punch down. Shape two (or just one big loaf in large pan) loaves and place into greased bread pans and let rise again to almost double in size. Then place pans into oven 375° F. for 30 - 45 minutes. Tap bottom - hollow sound means it's done. Cool and enjoy.

PASSOVER ROLLS

Mildred Auerbach

2 C. matzoh meal
½ tsp. salt
1 T. sugar

1 C. water
½ C. vegetable oil
4 eggs

Combine matzoh meal with salt and sugar. Bring oil and water to a boil. Add to matzoh meal mixture and mix well. Beat in eggs thoroughly, one at a time. Allow to stand 15 minutes. With oiled hands shape into rolls and place on a well-greased cookie sheet. Bake in a moderate oven 375° for 50 minutes or until golden brown. Makes 12 rolls.

"CHOCOLATE" (CAROB) RYE BREAD

Leslie Ann Hogan

A flat bread that looks and tastes like pumpernickel, but without wheat, yeast, sugar, corn or chocolate, for folks with those food sensitivities or allergies. Also good for those on anti-Candida diet. Makes one small loaf.

DRY:
1½ C. rye flour*
2 T. oat bran
¼ C. uncooked rolled oats**
(oatmeal) to bring flour mixture
    to 2 C.
½ tsp. salt
2 tsp. baking powder

1 T. caraway seeds 2 T. carob powder
½ tsp. ground fenugreek (if available)

LIQUID:
 1 egg beaten
2 T. vegetable oil (safflower or canola)
water
¼ C. cooked oatmeal**

*Or use other flours: soy, millet, quinoa, buckwheat with rye. Remember to keep proportion: 2 C. flour mixture to 1 C. liquid mixture. Experiment!
**This recipe can be made either with uncooked oats or cooked oatmeal. If using uncooked rolled oats, dry flour should measure 2 C.; if using cooked oat meal, dry flour should measure 1¾ C.

Oil and flour a baking sheet or (what I use) 10" cast iron frying pan. In a large bowl combine dry ingredients. In smaller bowl combine liquid ingredients. (Liquid ingredients together should measure one cup. If using cooked oatmeal add to egg, oil and water to equal one cup.)

Add liquid mixture to dry ingredients. Stir until mixed. Dough will be stiff. (Easiest to stir with wooden spoon.) Roll dough ball onto floured pan using wooden spoon and rubber spatula.

Flour hands and pat down dough to a round or square 1" thick. Cut cross on top. Preheat oven to 450°. Bake 20 - 30 minutes. Insert paring knife in thickest part after 20 minutes to test for moisture. Test every few minutes until knife comes out dry. Loaf will be about 1¼" high. Let cool on wire rack.

ZUCCHINI QUICK BREAD

Floyd Blaisdell

½ C. flour
½ tsp. baking soda
⅛ tsp. baking powder
1 tsp. cinnamon
½ C. light veg. oil or sweet butter

½ tsp. salt
2 eggs
½ tsp. vanilla extract
1 C. shredded zucchini
½ C. organic raisins

Mix all dry ingredients together in a bowl. In another bowl, mix all wet ingredients. Add dry ingredients to the second bowl, stir 2 minutes. Pour batter into baking pan. Bake at 350° for 50 - 60 minutes until top is springy to touch.

AUNT NORA'S IRISH SODA BREAD

Hon. Thomas J. Manton

2½ C. white flour
2 tsp. baking powder
½ tsp. salt
1 C. raisins

2 oz. butter
¾ C. sugar
2 eggs
1 C. buttermilk at room temperature

Preheat oven to 350°. Mix together flour, baking powder, salt and raisins. In a large mixing bowl, mix together the butter and sugar. Add eggs. Gradually add the flour mixture, alternating with the buttermilk. Shape with hands and place on baking sheet. Bake at 350° for 1 hour or less.

RAISIN CURRANT BREAD

Nicholas DiBrino

6 C. sifted all-purpose flour	¾ C. currants
1 tsp. ground cinnamon	¾ C. raisins
½ tsp. ground nutmeg	2 lg. eggs
2 tsp. baking powder	3 C. milk
1 tsp. salt	6 T. grated orange rind
1½ C. granulated sugar	½ C. unsalted butter, melted & cooled

Lightly grease 3 loaf pans and line with parchment or wax paper. In a large bowl put the first 6 ingredients. Set aside. In a second bowl combine raisins and currants and mix with 1 T. of mixture from bowl #1. In a third bowl mix remaining ingredients together. Make a well in center of ingredients in large bowl and pour in egg and milk mixture from third bowl. Sprinkle with raisins and currants. Combine all ingredients together with a wooden spoon till just blended. Pour and scrape batter into 3 pans. Bake in a preheated oven at 325° for 45 to 50 minutes. Test with a toothpick. When toothpick comes out clean, cake is baked. DO NOT OVER BAKE! Makes three 3½×7½" loaves.

BAGELS

Ben the Baker

4½ C. all-purpose flour	1½ C. warm water
2 pkgs. active dry yeast	4 T. sugar
1 T. salt	

In a large bowl, mix 1½ cups all-purpose flour and 2 packages active dry yeast. Combine 1½ cups warm water (110°), 3 T. sugar, and 1 T. salt; add to flour mixture. Beat at low speed of electric mixer for 30 seconds, scraping sides of bowl. Beat 3 minutes at high speed. By hand, stir in 3 cups all-purpose flour to make a moderately stiff dough. Knead on lightly floured surface till smooth (8 to 10 minutes). Cover; let rest 15 minutes.

Cut dough into 12 portions; shape into balls. Punch a hole in centers of each. Pull gently to enlarge hole, working into uniform shape. Cover; let rise 20 minutes.

In kettle, bring 1 gallon water and 1 T. sugar to a boil. Simmer 4 bagels at a time for 7 minutes, turning once. Drain. Place on a greased baking sheet. Bake at 375° for 30 to 35 minutes. Makes 12 bagels.

Or - Go to a bagel store!

IRISH SODA BREAD

Rita Gormley

4 C. flour
½ C. sugar
¼ tsp. baking soda
2 T. baking powder
½ tsp. salt

1 C. raisins
2 T. caraway seeds
2 eggs
1½ C. buttermilk
1 stick (8 T.) butter

Preheat oven to 350°. In a large bowl mix the flour, sugar, baking soda, baking powder and salt. Toss with a wooden fork, add raisins and caraway seeds. Put eggs, buttermilk, and butter in a blender and mix for about 30 seconds, 3 times. Pour into the dry mixture a little at a time. Blend well with a spoon or fork. Dough should be heavy and not wet. Dust hands with flour and mold dough into a round. Put into greased 9" round pan. Dust the top generously with flour. Use the wrong end of fork to put a deep cross into the dough. Bake for 1 hour. Cool on rack. To freeze, wrap in foil.

IRISH SODA BREAD

Cathy Brady

4 C. flour
4 tsp. baking powder
1 scant tsp. baking soda
1 C. sugar
2 C. raisins

½ pt. sour cream
½ pt. milk
2 eggs
½ tsp. salt

Mix dry ingredients. In separate bowl mix eggs, milk, sour cream. Pour and blend with dry ingredients. Place in a greased floured bundt pan. Bake at 350° for 45 -50 minutes. Enjoy!

BLUEBERRY LEMON LOAF

Jill Rosenfeld

2 C. unsifted all-purpose flour
1½ tsp. baking powder
¼ tsp. salt
½ C. butter
1 C. sugar
2 eggs
⅓ C. milk

2 tsp. grated lemon peel
heaping ½ C. walnuts or hazelnuts or pecans
1 C. fresh blueberries
GLAZE: ¼ C. fresh lemon juice
⅓ C. sugar

Lightly grease a loaf pan. Preheat oven to 350°. Sift dry ingredients together. Cream butter and sugar until fluffy, add eggs, one at a time, beating well after each addition. Add dry ingredients alternately with milk to creamed-egg mixture. Beat until well combined. Stir in lemon peel, chopped nuts and blueberries. Turn into buttered pan. Bake at 350° for 55 - 60 minutes. Do not over bake.

Glaze while still warm: Poke top with toothpick. Stir lemon juice and sugar over medium heat until hot and sugar is dissolved. Brush at once over baked loaf. Cool 10 minutes before removing from pan.

SCONES

Kay Pacher

2 C. flour, sifted
1 T. baking powder
2 T. sugar
½ tsp. salt

½ C. raisins
1 lg. egg
¼ C. salad oil
¼ C. evaporated milk

Mix dry ingredients together, adding raisins. Beat egg, then mix well with milk and oil. Pour wet mixture into the dry mixture and mix together with a fork. Flour a board or your kitchen table. Place dough on it and knead well, 5 or 10 minutes. Divide into two equal parts. Shape each into a circle ½" thick. Cut each circle into 12 wedges. Place on ungreased fry-pan or griddle, fry 6 to 10 minutes on each side, till golden brown. You have 2 dozen scones.

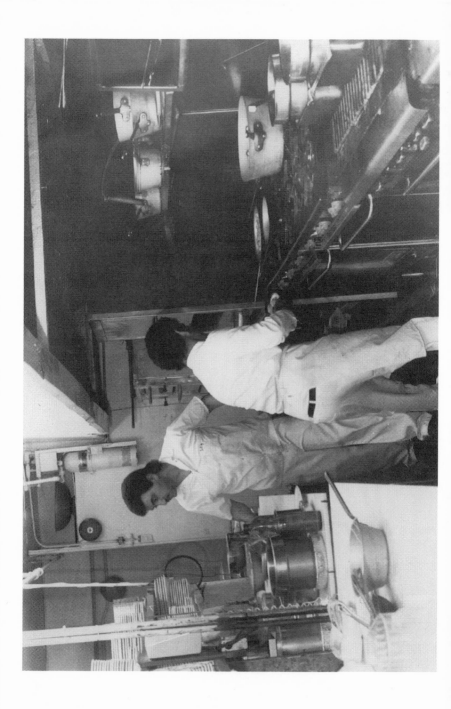

MAIN DISHES

Tomatoes With Pesto Topping
Stuffed Potatoes
Broiled Potatoes
Throggs Neck Mickies (Potatoes)
Macaroni & Cheese
Macaroni & Cheese Variant
Mike's Chili
Chili
Barry's Chili
Pizza Rustica (Meat and Cheese Pie)
Mike's Pizza Rustica
Tony's Pride Pizza
Ground Beef and Noodle Casserole
Best Tuna Casserole
Meat & Pasta Fast Baked Ziti
Empanadas
(Spanish Style Beef Patties)
Mulligatawny
Black Beans (Eclectic Caribbean Style)
Puerto Rican Pork Pies
Chop Suey

Zuppa De Pesce Roma
Matt's Ratatouille
Paella
Spanish Paella
Goulash
Tiropeta (Cheese Pie)
Spanacopita (Spinach Pie)
Huevos Rancheros
Spanish Omelet (Tortilla Espanola)
Frittata (Flat Omelet)
Crabmeat Quiche
Cheese Tortellini with Cream &
Walnut Sauce
Bow Ties à la Caruso
Pasta Pesto
Broccoli Rabe with Shrimp over
Pasta
Pasta & Broccoli with Anchovy
Sauce
Linguine and Shrimp
Arroz Con Pollo

Kitchen of Alex & Henry's Restaurant, 862 Courtlandt Avenue at 160th Street, May 1989. This restaurant has served Italian cuisine in the same location for over 50 years. It expanded to an additional location in Westchester.

The Bronx County Historical Society Research Library and Archives

22621B-ca

TOMATOES WITH PESTO TOPPING

Jill Rosenfeld

3 med. size ripe tomatoes
1 C. fresh breadcrumbs
fresh pesto sauce (see below)

½ C. extra toasted pinenuts
extra Parmesan cheese

Cut tomatoes in half horizontally, squeeze out seeds and remove the top part of the tomato flesh (stem area). Mix breadcrumbs with enough pesto sauce to make a thick paste and add pinenuts. Spread equally on top of tomato halves. Place tomato halves on a baking sheet lined with foil. Bake in 350° oven for 12 - 15 minutes. Top with extra Parmesan and broil until just browned on top. Serve warm or at room temperature.

PESTO SAUCE
2 cloves garlic
3 oz. grated Parmesan cheese
¼ C. toasted pinenuts
2 C. fresh basil leaves or combination

½ basil and ½ parsley
1 tsp. salt
¼ C. olive oil
¾ C. safflower oil

Process everything except oil in food processor. With the machine running, add oils gradually and blend well. Makes approximately 2 cups.

STUFFED POTATOES

Laura Hirshman

4 lg. baking potatoes
½ stick butter
¼ C. milk

chicken giblets, cooked, minced fine
salt and pepper
1 egg yolk, beaten

Bake the potatoes until done. Cut a "cap" from the top of each potato and scoop out the inside carefully and mash with butter and milk. Season the minced chicken giblets with pepper and salt, stir into the potatoes and the beaten egg yolk. Heat in a saucepan until very hot, fill the skins, replace the tops, and set in oven for 3 minutes.

BROILED POTATOES

Ken Clanton

3 or 4 lg. boiled potatoes, cold   salt and pepper
2 T. butter   1 tsp. minced parsley

Slice the cold boiled potatoes lengthwise in rather thick pieces. Broil potatoes in buttered pan at 325 - 350°, stirring occasionally. When golden brown, remove from broiler, butter all over, salt and pepper, serve very hot. A nicer way of dressing them is to beat up a spoonful of butter into cream with a spoonful of minced parsley and spread on each potato slice.

THROGGS NECK MICKIES (POTATOES)

Geri Olbermann

Potatoes, large, unwashed, as many as needed

1. Build a large bonfire with paper, twigs, and any unpainted wood or material that will burn. (Painted wood may give off harmful chemicals)
2. When fire is burning brightly, deposit potatoes in firebed.
3. A twig can be used to test when done, or you can rely on the delicious aroma of roasting potatoes that permeates the air.
4. Especially delicious when entire potato is eaten, charred crispy skin and all.
5. Served without any other accompaniments or enhancements.
6. Enjoyed all year round, but especially during and after sledding on Lawton Hill, on cold, wintry nights in Throggs Neck, The Bronx, New York.

NOTE: Potatoes had to be smuggled out of the kitchen in some instances, in order to introduce friends to this culinary delight. Knowing this, mothers usually tried to have a good supply of potatoes on hand at all times, and sometimes would prepare some hot chocolate, that is, if we shared a potato with them!

MACARONI & CHEESE

Phyllis Carile

1 lb. elbow macaroni
1 lb. Kraft Old English Sharp Cheddar cheese (shredded)
6 C. milk
¼ lb. margarine (plus some for coating

baking dish)
1 heaping T. flour
breadcrumbs
salt & pepper

Preheat oven 350°. Coat large baking dish with margarine and breadcrumbs. Put milk and margarine in pot. Add a little water to flour to make a smooth paste and add to milk mixture. When all is dissolved, add cheese and continue to stir to a slight boil. Set aside.

Cook macaroni: when it comes to a boil, only cook 2 more minutes. Drain pasta and mix with cheese mixture. Pour into baking dish, sprinkle top with breadcrumbs. Bake for ½ hour.

MACARONI & CHEESE VARIANT

Kay Pacher

½ lb. macaroni - elbows, wagon wheels, or similar
8 oz. Velveeta processed American

cheese - loaf form
1 can Campbell's tomato soup

Put macaroni in pot with water, set to boil. Cut up cheese into ¼" cubes. Set aside enough cubes to spread out on top. Open can of soup. Do not add anything to it. Grease inside of a 2-qt. Pyrex baking dish. When macaroni is done (not too soft), drain off water. Empty macaroni into baking dish. Put cubes (except those saved for topping) into macaroni and mix well till melted. Now empty tomato soup into macaroni and cheese and mix well. Scatter remaining cheese cubes on top and place in a 350° oven. Bake about ½ hour, when cheese on top should be forming a nice crust. Serve with a salad and you have a tasty meal.

MIKE'S CHILI

Katherine Morris Allan

1 lb. ground meat
1 med. onion chopped
2 (15 oz.) cans chili beans - undrained

1 can tomato soup - condensed
1 envelope taco seasoning
½ C. water approx.

Brown meat & onion. Add other ingredients. Simmer uncovered ½ hour or more.

CHILI

Michele Franich

2 lbs. chopped chuck
4 lg. cans red chili beans
4 (6 oz.) cans tomato sauce
4 - 6 T. chili powder

1 T. onion powder
1 T. garlic powder to taste
1 T. pepper to taste
2 tsp. soy sauce or to taste

Brown meat in dutch oven. Drain off fat. Add chili beans and tomato sauce.
Add next 5 ingredients and mix well. Cover and simmer for approx. 2 hours.
Correct seasonings - and - Enjoy.

BARRY'S CHILI

Barry Telphy

1 lb. hamburger meat
2 tsp. olive oil
1 green pepper
4 scallions

1 lb. tomato sauce
1 lb. can kidney beans
1 tsp. chili powder
½ tsp. salt

Put olive oil in saucepan and cook up meat, chopped pepper and scallions until
brown. Remove the fat. Add tomato sauce, kidney beans, chili powder and salt.
Stir and cook until it boils and then simmer for 10 - 15 minutes.

PIZZA RUSTICA (MEAT AND CHEESE PIE)

Laura Tosi

I make it for Easter and Christmas in a 7×12×½" baking dish.

DOUGH
3 C. all-purpose flour
2 tsp. baking powder
½ tsp. salt
½ C. shortening (Crisco) or lard
3 lg. eggs at room temperature, beaten
  lightly
4 T. cold water
GLAZE
1 lg. egg, beaten lightly with pinch of
salt

FILLING
2 lbs. ricotta cheese
1 lb. shredded mozzarella
¼ C. grated locatelli cheese
salt and pepper to taste
⅓ C. coarsely chopped fresh parsley
7 lg. eggs, beat lightly
¼ lb. Sicilian salami
¼ lb. diced pepperoni or dried sausage
3 oz. prosciutto - have it cut in one
piece, trim fat and dice

Preheat oven to 375°
1. Combine all the dry ingredients for dough in a large bowl. Cut in shortening until mixture gets crumbly. Beat in eggs and cold water alternately, a tablespoonful at a time, until it makes a ball. Wrap dough in plastic wrap and put in refrigerator. (You can even make the dough a day ahead and keep in refrigerator.)
2. Combine all of the ingredients for the filling in a large bowl, set it aside.
3. Remove the dough from the refrigerator and divide into thirds. Combine 2 of the pieces and roll them out onto a lightly floured surface into a rectangular shape ⅛", approximately 11×16".
4. Fold dough in half. Carefully lift and place in baking dish 7×12×½". Press dough onto the sides and bottom of dish, leave a 1" overhang. Spread filling evenly over the dough.
5. Roll remaining piece of dough onto a lightly floured surface, also rectangular shape ⅛" thick. Place dough over the filling and pinch the overhang edges together with your thumb and forefinger to make the crust edge. Now brush the top with the glaze and prick it all over with a fork 20 - 25 times.
6. Bake 1 hour and 30 minutes, or until it is golden brown. Place the Pizza Rustica on a rack and let it cool for approximately 3 hours (the top crust will be puffed up but settles while it is cooling). If it will be eaten within 24 hours, it does not have to be refrigerated, just cover with a towel.

MIKE'S PIZZA RUSTICA

Buona Pasqua

This recipe makes one 10" pie and one 8" pie.

CRUST:
4 C. flour
1⅓ sticks of butter
¼ C. sugar
4 eggs
1 T. lemon rind

CENTER:
12 eggs (put aside two egg whites)
¾ C. grated Locatelli/Romano cheese

2 T. chopped parsley
1 tsp. black pepper
2 T. sugar
1 lg. sopressata
1 lg. dry sausage
1 lb. prosciutto (¼" slices)
1½ lbs. Bertolli table cheese
1½ lbs. fresh basket cheese
3 lbs. ricotta cheese

For the crust, make a well in the flour, place all other crust ingredients into the center of the well. Mix well. Knead until smooth. Divide according to size of pan. (For two pie crusts and tops.)

For the center filling, cube cheese and cold cuts into chunks (not diced). Mix the ricotta cheese and chunks together. In a separate bowl, beat all other ingredients together well, then add the chunks. Pour the mixture into dough-lined pan, add top crust, close edges well, make slits on top. Brush with beaten egg whites. Bake for approximately 1 to 1½ hours. Test with a toothpick or watch that juices on top of pie evaporate. Let cool and refrigerate overnight ... che buono!

TONY'S PRIDE PIZZA

Anthony R. Morante

1 C. water
1 packet or small block of yeast
1 pinch sugar
few drops of oil
3 C. flour or gluten
salt and pepper
16 oz. plum tomatoes

fresh basil
8 oz. mozzarella, shredded
1 sm. boiled potato
Parmesan cheese
rosemary or thyme
2 garlic cloves, chopped

Combine water, yeast, sugar and oil. Stir until yeast is dissolved. Pour contents into 1 cup of the sifted flour with a pinch of salt and pepper; stir vigorously or combine in food processor with pulsing action. Add remainder of flour and boiled potato into the bowl. Stir or pulsate until ingredients do not stick to spatula or mixing disc. Knead dough with balls of hand in outward motion for about 1 minute. Let dough rise in greased bowl for about 1 hour.

Lay out dough in 2×13" round pan and let rise for another hour.

Place shredded mozzarella evenly over the dough. Pour the tomatoes over cheese including the herbs and garlic. Sprinkle Parmesan over pizza. Place in preheated oven at 425° for about 15 minutes or until you see the cheese starting to brown.

GROUND BEEF AND NOODLE CASSEROLE

Vivian Aitken Mall

1½ lb. ground beef
1 lb. curly noodles
1 C. ketchup

2 (8 oz.) cans tomato sauce
¼ tsp. pepper
4 oz. shredded cheddar cheese

Cook noodles as directed on package, and drain. Brown meat, add ketchup, tomato sauce and pepper. Combine noodles and meat mixture. Put in a 2-qt. casserole greased. Top with shredded cheese. Cook 25 minutes in 325° oven.

BEST TUNA CASSEROLE

Elizabeth J. Hall

1 can water packed solid white tuna*
1 med. onion, sliced paper thin and chopped fine
2 stalks celery, cut paper thin
½ bell pepper, green, red or mixed, sliced thin
4 slices white bread cut in ½" dice

1 egg, beaten with a smidgen of water
⅛ C. cooking sherry or dry sherry
3 T. whole milk
½ C. mayonnaise
⅜ C. breadcrumbs
2 T. butter or margarine

*Or you can substitute salmon, shrimp or whatever you like.

Drain tuna* and cut or flake to your choice. Into the tuna, toss onion, celery and pepper with bread cubes and half of the mayonnaise. At this time add your choice of seasonings and salt and pepper. Toss this mixture until well mixed.

Prepare casserole dish by coating with Pam or other cooking oil. Put the mixture into the casserole dish. Place butter or margarine in small shallow pan and heat until quite soft. Spread over mixture in casserole dish. Bake in 350° oven for 1 hour.

MEAT & PASTA FAST BAKED ZITI

Jacqueline Kutner

1 box ziti macaroni
1 30-oz jar of sauce (Ragu or Prego)
1½ lb. ground beef or veal
¼ tsp. pepper

salt, &/or Italian seasoning, &/or garlic powder
8 oz. grated mozzarella cheese

Mix ¼ tsp. pepper into the meat. Then add ½ tsp. of each of the other spices and mix into the meat. Form into meatballs and saute them in frying pan till browned. Cook pasta *al dente* (firm). Drain. Add sauce and meatballs, mix well. In a large baking pan, place a layer of macaroni and meatballs about 2 - 3" deep. Sprinkle mozzarella cheese over it, about ½" deep. Repeat layers. Top layer should be generously sprinkled with cheese and sauce. Bake at 350° till the cheese bubbles. Serve with salad and garlic bread. Buon appetito! Enjoy!

EMPANADAS (SPANISH STYLE BEEF PATTIES)

Margie Menendez

Approx. 2 - 3 T. oil (enough to saute onion and pepper)
1 med. onion, chopped
1 sm. green pepper, chopped
2 pieces of garlic, crushed
1 T. Spanish parsley "cilantro" (chopped)
1 T. chopped olives
salt to taste
black pepper to taste
½ tsp. oregano
¼ tsp. ground cumin
8 oz. tomato sauce
1 lb. ground beef
1 pkg. frozen "Goya" Empanada discs (approx. 10/pkg.)
OPTIONAL: mozzarella cheese
Oil for frying

Cook onion and green pepper in oil until tender. Add garlic, parsley and olives; stir and cook about 1 minute. Add salt, black pepper, oregano, cumin; stir, wait a few seconds and then add tomato sauce. Cook about 3 minutes. Add chopped meat; stir, cover and simmer for about 10 minutes, stirring frequently. Drain this meat stuffing, leaving some sauce so that meat does not dry up, or simply keep saucepan tilted. Stuff discs with approximately 1 heaping T. of meat and seal the edges with a fork. (OPTIONAL: Before sealing the patties, you can add cubed mozzarella cheese.) Fry in very hot oil until golden.

MULLIGATAWNY

Gobba O'Connor Beirne

1 chopped onion
½ tsp. curry powder
1 C. diced chicken or
    1 lb. beef stew meat
1 apple, peeled and chopped
2 chopped carrots
2 C. chopped celery
1 chopped green pepper
sprinkle flour
4 C. chicken broth
2 peeled tomatoes
1 tsp. parsley
dash of lemon juice
1 tsp. sugar

In a large pan, cook onion until tender, with curry powder. Stir in beef/chicken, apple, carrots, celery, green pepper. Cook for 5 minutes. Sprinkle flour over beef/chicken-vegetable mixture, mix well. Stir in broth, tomatoes, parsley, lemon juice, sugar, salt, and pepper, to taste. Bring to a boil, stir to prevent burning, reduce heat and simmer, covered, for 30 minutes.

BLACK BEANS (ECLECTIC CARIBBEAN STYLE)

Ricardo R. Fernández

(Editor's Note: Ricardo R. Fernández is President of Herbert H. Lehman College, The City University of New York. He informs us that this is truly an eclectic recipe that has evolved over the past twenty years and includes suggestions and hints from various recipes by many others, including salsa singer and actor Rubén Blades.)

1 lb. dried black beans, washed (or 3 cans - each 14 oz.- of cooked beans in water)
1 can (46 oz.) chicken broth (water and chicken bouillon cubes - one per cup- may be substituted)

½ tsp. dried oregano
¼ tsp. ground cumin
1 bay leaf
1 small jar sweet red pimentos
   (chopped) and accompanying liquid
2-3 T. balsamic vinegar
2 T. dry red wine (burgundy, merlot or
   chianti)
1 tsp. sugar
¼ C. olive oil

salt and pepper to taste
SOFRITO:
2-3 strips bacon, sliced small
1 slice boiled ham, finely cut
3-4 cloves garlic, minced
1 medium green pepper (cored and
   seeded), diced
1 medium onion, diced
½ bunch cilantro (Chinese parsley),
   finely chopped (leaves and stem)

1. Soak beans overnight in cold water; discard water, set aside in 8 qt. pot.
2. Prepare SOFRITO as follows:
   a. Fry cut bacon strips in a pan at medium heat until crisp; add
      chopped ham and stir fry 1 minute.
   b. Add garlic, green pepper, onion, cilantro. Saute until soft but not brown.
3. Add SOFRITO to beans and add 4 cups of chicken broth. Mix well. (If using canned beans in water, add 3 cans of chicken broth.)
4. Add all remaining ingredients (oregano, cumin, bay leaf, pimentos, balsamic vinegar, wine, sugar, cilantro and olive oil); add salt and pepper to taste.
5. Simmer uncovered over a slow fire for 2 -3 hours, until beans are cooked through and the liquid thickens. Add more chicken broth, as needed, if liquid is too thick.
6. Serve over white rice or alone (in soup bowls, with chopped sweet red onion, a dollop of sour cream and a sprig of cilantro). Serves 8.

NOTE: Beans taste better if prepared the day before and reheated, but they may be served on the same day. Recipe may be doubled easily for a larger party or increased proportionately with no change in flavor. Avocado slices go well with this dish.

PUERTO RICAN PORK PIES

Julio Diaz

2 C. flour
½ tsp. baking soda
¼ C. butter
2 egg yolks
1 T. cooking oil
½ lb. ground pork
½ C. chopped onion
1 clove garlic, minced
1 hard cooked egg, chopped

¼ tsp. dried oregano, crushed
¼ tsp. dried red pepper flakes, crushed
½ of a 6-oz. can tomato paste
¼ C. raisins
1 T. snipped parsley
1 T. capers
2 tsp. vinegar
2 T. chopped pitted ripe olives

Stir together flour, baking soda, and 1 tsp. salt. Cut in butter till the size of small peas. Combine eggs and ½ cup water; add to flour mixture. Stir till it clings together; form into a ball. Cover; refrigerate 1 hour. Meanwhile, heat oil in skillet. Cook pork, onion, garlic, oregano, dried red pepper, ½ tsp. salt, and ⅛ tsp. pepper till meat is browned and onion is tender. Stir in tomato paste, raisins, parsley, capers, vinegar, and ¼ cup water. Simmer, covered, for 5 minutes. Remove from heat. Stir in hard cooked egg and chopped ripe olives.

On a lightly floured surface, roll one quarter of the dough at a time to 1/16" thickness. Cut into 3" circles. Place 1 tsp. meat mixture in the center of each circle. Fold over. Moisten edges and seal well, using tines of a fork.
Fry a few at a time in deep hot fat (350°) till golden, about 3 minutes. -Or- Place on a greased baking pan. Bake at 425° till browned, 10 to 12 minutes. Makes about 48 meat pies.

CHOP SUEY

Anthony Parisse

2 C. cooked pork, cut in
    slices ¼" wide
½ C. celery
1 C. green onion
½ C. green pepper
1 C. mushrooms
1 C. bean sprouts

2 T. cooking oil
½ C. peeled tomatoes
1 C. strong chicken consomme
salt and pepper
1 T. soy sauce
3 T. dry sherry
cornstarch (if needed)

Stir fry the onion and celery in oil for 3 - 5 minutes. Add the mushrooms, pepper and bean sprouts, and stir fry for 2 - 3 minutes. Add the pork, tomatoes, consomme, soy sauce, sherry, salt and pepper. Thicken with cornstarch, if needed. Remove from pan or wok and serve.

ZUPPA DE PESCE ROMA

Chef Rodneey DiBenedetto

4 little neck clams
6 - 8 med. shrimp
6 - 8 scallops
2 Maryland hard shell crabs or 2
   halves of snow crab legs
8-10 mussels
1 med. deboned fish fillet, your choice
2 lobster tails (med.)
1 lb. angel hair pasta
1½ C. tomato sauce

2 whole cloves of garlic
2 - 3 bay leaves
1 T. oregano
1 T. basil
1 T. thyme
½ - 1 C. red wine
salt & pepper to taste
OPTIONAL: Hot Sauce 1½ tsp. or to
taste

STEP 1: In a large pot of water (5 - 6 C.), add a little oil and salt to prepare the angel hair pasta. Bring to a boil until 90% done. Set aside.
STEP 2: In a large skillet (with lid) heat 1 T. olive oil, add garlic (finely chopped). Saute until brown, add tomato sauce (and hot sauce if desired) and crabs. Wait 20 seconds and add lobster and clams, mussels, shrimp, and whole fish fillet draped across the middle. Add wine and seasonings, leaving skillet lid slightly ajar. Cook over low flame approximately 15 - 20 minutes or until clams and mussels fully open.

Drain pasta and make a bed in a large platter. Place equal portion of seafood on each side of platter. Serve with garlic bread, Italian bread or rolls.

MATT'S RATATOUILLE

Katherine Morris Allan

3 zucchini cut into 1½" quarters
3 onions sliced into short chunks
4 green peppers sliced into 1" pieces
2 or 3 cloves of garlic
4 shakes of Italian seasoning

1 lb. plum, no-salt tomatoes
1 bunch celery cut into 2 pieces
1 oz. white vinegar
white pepper to taste

Combine all ingredients in large pot, cook covered, on low heat, for 45 minutes.

PAELLA

Gary Morales

1 C. olive oil
2 med. sized onions
1 lg. green pepper
1 (2 lb.) chicken, cut in 8 pieces
2 cans jumbo shrimp
1 can spiced lobster
1 can clams
1 can tuna
¼ lb. diced, uncooked ham

¼ lb. pork, cut in chunks
1 can tomato sauce
1 can sweet red pimentos
1½ T. salt
1 tsp. garlic powder
½ tsp. paprika
4 C. chicken broth
2 C. canilla rice
1 can green peas

In large saucepan with tight-fitting cover, heat oil and brown lightly onions and green peppers. Add chicken, all seafood, ham and pork. Saute, stirring occasionally, until slightly golden. Add tomato sauce, 2 ground pimentos, salt, garlic powder, paprika. Allow to boil for 5 minutes; then add broth and continue to cook until chicken is tender. Add rice; cover tightly and allow to boil over low heat until rice is done and all water is absorbed. Serve garnished with green peas and remaining sweet red pimentos. Serves 8.

SPANISH PAELLA

Charles Salkow

¼ C. all-purpose flour
1 tsp. salt, dash of pepper
1 broiler-fryer chicken, 2½ to 3 lbs.,
    ready-to-cook, cut up
¼ C. olive oil
2½ C. chicken broth
2 med. onions, quartered
2 carrots, sliced (¾ C.)
⅔ C. regular rice

½ C. chopped celery with leaves
¼ C. chopped canned pimiento
1 clove garlic, minced
½ tsp. salt
½ tsp. dried oregano, crushed
¼ tsp. ground saffron
12 oz. shelled shrimp
12 small fresh clams in shells, washed
1 (9-oz.) pkg. frozen artichoke hearts

Combine flour, 1 tsp. salt, and pepper, and coat chicken with mixture. Brown chicken in olive oil for 20 minutes. Drain off excess fat; return all chicken to pan. Add chicken broth, onions, carrots, rice, celery, pimiento, garlic, ½ tsp. salt, oregano, and saffron. Simmer, covered, for ½ hour.

Add shrimp, clams, and artichokes. Simmer, covered, for ¼ hour.

GOULASH

H. Hertzberg

2 lbs. boneless beef chuck, cut in 1"
    cubes
3 T. cooking oil
1 (14-oz.) can beef broth
1 C. chopped onion
1 sm. green pepper, chopped
2 T. tomato paste

2 T. paprika
2 tsp. caraway seed
salt and pepper
⅓ C. cold water
3 T. flour
broad noodles
OPTIONAL: dairy sour cream

In large saucepan, brown beef cubes in hot oil. Add beef broth, onion, green pepper, tomato paste, paprika, caraway seed, ½ tsp. salt, and ¼ tsp. pepper. Blend cold water into flour. Stir into beef mixture. Simmer, covered, till meat is tender, about 1½ hours; stir occasionally. Serve over broad noodles. Sour cream as a garnish is optional. Serves 8.

TIROPETA (CHEESE PIE)

Kathryn Economides

1 lb. feta cheese
4 - 8 oz. pkgs. cream cheese
6 eggs

1 lb. filo dough
1 C. melted butter

Mix the feta cheese, cream cheese and eggs together, beating until smooth. Lay out filo dough one sheet at a time into a 13×15" baking pan and brush entire sheet with butter. Use half the filo dough for the bottom, fill with mixture, smooth out.

Use remaining filo dough for the top, remembering to butter every sheet. When finished, score the top into 2" square pieces. Sprinkle top with water and bake at 325° for 45 minutes lightly browned on top. Let cool and serve.

SPANACOPITA (SPINACH PIE)

Kathryn Economides

4 (8 oz.) pkgs. frozen chopped
spinach, drained
1 bunch scallions, chopped
1 onion, chopped
1 C. oil
1 lb. feta cheese

4 (8-oz.) pkgs. cream cheese
6 eggs
dill to taste
salt to taste
1 lb. filo dough
1 C. melted butter

In a pan cook spinach, scallions, onion and oil until onion and scallions are transparent. Remove from heat, let stand. In a bowl, mix feta cheese, cream cheese and eggs till smooth. Add the spinach mixture, mix together, add dill and salt to taste. Lay out filo dough in 13×15" pan, brush the entire sheet with melted butter. Repeat this until half the dough has been used. Add mixture, smooth it out so that it covers the pan. Add remaining filo dough, remember to butter every sheet when finished. Score the top into 2" pieces, sprinkle with water. Bake at 325° for 45 min. or until golden brown on top. Cool and serve.

HUEVOS RANCHEROS

Bradley Fenton

¼ C. cooking oil
6 flour tortillas
½ C. chopped onion
1 sm. clove garlic
3 lg. tomatoes

2 chopped green chili peppers
¼ tsp. salt
6 eggs
1 C. shredded Monterey Jack cheese

In a medium skillet, heat the ¼ C. cooking oil. Dip the tortillas in oil for a few seconds till softened but not brown. Keep warm. In the same skillet, cook the onion and garlic till tender but not brown (add more oil if necessary). Stir in the tomatoes, green chili peppers, and salt. Simmer, uncovered, 10 minutes. Slide the eggs into the hot tomato mixture, taking care not to break the egg yolks. Season the mixture with salt and pepper. Cover skillet and cook the eggs till of desired doneness. Place an egg with some of the tomato mixture on each tortilla. Top each serving with a small amount of shredded cheese. Serves 6.

SPANISH OMELET (TORTILLA ESPANOLA)

Carmela Santiago

1 (24 oz.) pkg. Ore-Ida potatoes with onions and peppers
4 tsp. oil

4 eggs
salt to taste

On a frying pan fry potatoes in oil until tender. Mix in a bowl 4 eggs, well beaten. Add potatoes and salt to taste. Place in a frying pan 3 minutes on one side. Turn over and leave 2 minutes on the other side. Serve hot or cold.

FRITTATA (FLAT OMELET)

Laura Tosi

2 med. sized potatoes
¼ C. green or red peppers or spinach
or any other vegetable of choice
(spinach should be boiled and drained)
¼ C. onions
4 eggs

¼ C. locatelli cheese
3 T. finely chopped parsley
4 T. coarse dried breadcrumbs
salt and pepper to taste
4 to 5 T. olive oil
1 garlic clove, minced
2 T. basil, finely chopped

1. Cut up potatoes in thin flat slices (not too thin), dice pepper and onions.
2. Beat eggs in a bowl, add cheese, parsley, breadcrumbs, add salt and pepper.
3. Heat the oil in a 9" nonstick skillet. Add the garlic and let it sizzle for a few seconds. Throw in the potatoes, onions and peppers (or patted dry spinach or other veggie of your choice). Cook for 3 minutes or until potatoes and peppers are soft, stirring regularly so that they do not stick.
4. Pour the egg mixture into pan and cook over a low heat until it sets. Shake pan gently from time to time and with a knife make sure the sides are not sticking. In 4 minutes or so the frittata should be fairly firm, though wet on top. Shaking the pan once again, put a waiting plate or flat pan on top of the frying pan and over the sink turn pan onto plate or flat pan, wet side down. Slide the frittata back into the frying pan and cook an additional 2 to 3 minutes. Slide the frittata onto a serving plate. Serves 3 or 4.

CRABMEAT QUICHE

Naomi Schildwachter Herron

3 eggs slightly beaten
1 C. sour cream
½ tsp. Worcestershire sauce
¾ tsp. salt
1 C. shredded Swiss cheese

1 can (7½ oz.) crabmeat, drained and
   flaked
1 can (3½ oz.) French fried onions
1 - 9" baked pastry shell

Heat oven to 300°. Combine eggs, sour cream, Worcestershire sauce and salt. Stir in cheese, crabmeat and fried onions. Pour into baked pastry shell. Bake 55 to 60 minutes or until custard is set and a silver knife inserted in the center comes out clean. Serves 8 to 10 as an appetizer.

CHEESE TORTELLINI WITH CREAM & WALNUT SAUCE

Martin D. Garry

1 lb. cheese tortellini
1 pt. heavy cream
¼ lb. butter or margarine

½ C. Parmesan cheese
pinch of nutmeg
1 C. walnuts, finely chopped

Cook pasta. While pasta is boiling, mix together the cream, butter, Parmesan cheese, and nutmeg. Heat mixture but do not boil. Drain the pasta and pour the sauce over the pasta. Serve individually with a sprinkle of walnuts and Parmesan cheese.

BOW TIES À LA CARUSO

Martin D. Garry

1 qt. chicken livers, cut into chunks
1 lb. bow ties - farfelle pasta
2 T. olive oil

2 lg. C. plum tomatoes
1 clove garlic, minced
1 sm. onion

In a frying pan, combine 2 T. of olive oil, minced garlic clove, and 1 small onion finely, chopped. Add 2 large cups of unpeeled plum tomatoes, chopped. In another pan, cook the chicken livers in butter for about 5 minutes. Combine all ingredients and simmer for 15 minutes. In a large pot, cook pasta *al dente;* drain, and pour sauce over the pasta. Serve with green salad and a hunk of round Italian bread.

PASTA PESTO

Patricia C. Merola

1 lb. spinach pasta
2 cloves garlic (should be fresh for proper taste)
4 bunches fresh basil
salt to taste

¾ C. olive oil
3 - 4 T. grated Parmesan cheese
1 sm. pkg. cream cheese
½ C. pignoli nuts (pine nuts) to taste

Wash the basil with cold water and prepare the garlic by peeling. Cook pasta. While the pasta is boiling, blend the basil, garlic, salt, and some of the oil in a blender or food processor. Then, add the Parmesan cheese and cream cheese, making a creamy, light green consistency as you add the rest of the oil to your taste. Do not cook or heat the final mixture. Spoon it over the hot spinach pasta immediately and serve it quickly. The pignoli nuts can be added right before eating. Also, any of your favorite pasta can be used.

NOTE: There are several American variations to this very popular Genovese recipe. However, there is one authentic Italian preparation, still used in and around Genoa, which calls for small white potatoes and long, uncut string beans to be added to the pesto. In addition, Pecorino (ewe's milk) cheese is always used in place of the Parmesan. Serve this with a bottle of light, dry, white wine - like a Roman Frascati - and the ordinary Tuesday becomes a holiday.

BROCCOLI RABE WITH SHRIMP OVER PASTA

Mike Greco

1 lb. bow ties - farfelle pasta
6 cloves garlic (whole)
¼ C. olive oil
1 lb. med. shrimp, peeled & deveined
1 lb. broccoli rabe, cleaned,

steamed and cut
1 sm. can clam juice
¼ C. fresh parsley
salt and pepper

Prepare pasta in boiling water (add salt to water and remove pasta *al dente*). saute garlic in olive oil. When garlic browns, add shrimp to skillet (cook shrimp quickly, do not overcook). When shrimp are partially cooked, add broccoli rabe and clam juice. Add majority of parsley, let simmer 5 minutes. Remove majority of mixture from skillet, leaving liquid in skillet. Add pasta, saute 2 minutes. Place in serving dish, top pasta with remaining mixture, garnish with parsley.

PASTA & BROCCOLI WITH ANCHOVY SAUCE

Geri Olbermann

3 lg. stalks broccoli
1 lb. macaroni (orecchiette, rotini, or shells)

1 clove garlic, crushed
2 tins of rolled anchovies
⅓ C. olive oil
OPTIONAL: Italian grating cheese

1. Clean, wash and chop broccoli
2. Boil broccoli in water until tender. Drain, saving the broccoli water.
3. Cook macaroni in broccoli water, adding additional water if necessary.
4. In frying pan, add olive oil, crushed garlic and anchovies, combining them to form a sauce.
5. Pour garlic/anchovy sauce over cooked broccoli and macaroni and mix well.
6. Serve immediately, with grated Italian cheese.

LINGUINE AND SHRIMP

Elizabeth Beirne

1 clove minced garlic
4 T. extra virgin olive oil
½ lb. med. shrimp,
    shelled and deveined
1 C. chopped Italian plum tomatoes
1 red pepper diced
⅓ C. white wine

¼ tsp. oregano
¼ tsp. basil
2 T. fresh parsley
¼ tsp. fresh pepper
1 lb. linguine
aged Parmesan cheese

To make sauce: Saute garlic in olive oil in a heavy skillet. After a minute or so, add shrimp until opaque and then add all the other ingredients (except linguine and Parmesan cheese) and simmer for 10 - 15 minutes. Cook linguine *al dente*, drain and mix together with the sauce. Sprinkle aged Parmesan cheese and enjoy!

ARROZ CON POLLO

Ivette Arroyo

1 whole chicken cut up
oil
½ C. of tomato sauce
2 envelopes Sazón
½ C. Spanish olives with capers

2 cilantro leaves
3 C. rice
3½ C. water
salt to taste

In a large pot pour in enough oil to cover the bottom of the pot. Over a medium flame, mix the tomato sauce, Sazón, olives, cilantro. Add the chicken and saute for about 5 minutes. Put in the 3 C. of rice and pour in the 3½ C. of water. Add salt to taste. When the water has been absorbed, stir everything together, lower the flame a bit, and cover pot. Check and stir every 15 minutes until rice and chicken are fully cooked. Cooking time: approx. 45 minutes.

NOTES

22621B-ca

MEATS, POULTRY, SEAFOOD

Bake All Day Bar-B-Q Beef
Grandmother's Pot Roast
True Ireland Corned Beef &
Cabbage
Marinated Beef Cubes
Sweet & Sour Pot Roast with
Ginger Snap Gravy
Meat Loaf
Pot Roast
Ultan's Salisbury Steaklets
Beef in Wine Sauce
Beef in Burgundy
Ultan's Steak Stew
Jaeger Schnitzel with Spaetzle
Jaeger Schnitzel
Spaetzle
Broiled Veal Chops
Veal Parmigiana Bianco
Stuffed Breast of Veal - Roasted
Fried Tripe
Braised Hot Pepper Pork Chops
Orange Flavored Pork
Pork Chops and Potatoes -
Steamed
Deviled Ham

Chicken Breasts with Mozzarella
Broiled Chicken (Deviled)
Chicken and Mushrooms Bennett
Chicken Creole
Chicken Florentine
Eva's Lemon Chicken
Chicken-n-Stuffing Scallop
Ooo La La Chicken
Chicken Asparagus Pinwheels
Helen Placko's Chicken Vegetable
Stew
Jamaican Curried Goat (or Lamb)
Stuffed Chicken June
Bronx Duck
Fish, Pan Fried
Fish and Chips
Fish in Wine Sauce
Bluefish Delight
Poached Codfish Steak
Stewed Eels, English Style
Soft Shell Crabs
Broiled Lobster
Broiled Shrimp with Garlic
Coconut-Beer Shrimp
Shrimp Cantonese

At the corner of Prospect Avenue and 151st Street about 1950, a Spanish American Restaurant served the local Puerto Rican community. A sign in the window advertised the appearance of three Latin bands at the Tropicana Club.

The Bronx County Historical Society Research Library and Archives

BAKE ALL DAY BAR-B-Q BEEF

Kevin Kelleher

5 - 6 lbs. chuck roast
3 C. ketchup
2 T. Worcestershire
1 T. vinegar
1 clove garlic minced

1 qt. Canada Dry ginger ale
1 lg. onion minced
½ tsp. pepper
½ tsp. dry mustard
dash lemon juice

Combine ingredients and pour over roast in large ovenproof roasting pan. Cover and bake at 300° for 6 - 8 hours until tender, turning occasionally. Pull apart with a fork to shred. Serve on buns.

GRANDMOTHER'S POT ROAST

Diane Schulder Abrams

7 lbs. first cut of brisket
3 - 4 onions
4 - 6 carrots

1 dozen dried pitied prunes
generous sprinkle of allspice
salt and pepper

Pre-heat oven to 375°. Sear meat on both sides in a roasting pan. Remove meat from oven and pan. Line bottom of pan with slices of onions. Place meat on top of onions. Add a dash of salt and pepper. Cut carrot in quarters. Place carrots and prunes on top of meat and add a generous sprinkle of allspice. Cover roasting pan. Roast in oven for approximately 3½ hours. Enough gravy will be produced. Add water as meat is roasting, if necessary. Slice when cold. Serves 8.

This recipe was handed down to me from my Grandmother. It's finger licking good!

TRUE IRELAND CORNED BEEF & CABBAGE

Nicholas DiBrino

3 lbs. corned beef
1 tsp. ground cloves - or less (to taste)
1 T. freshly ground pepper, or less (to taste)

3 bay leaves
1 T. dry mustard
1 head of white cabbage, 1½ - 2 lbs., cut in 8 sections

Place corned beef and all seasonings in large pot. Cover with water. Bring slowly to boil. Cover and simmer gently for 1 hour. After 1 hour, add cabbage. Simmer for 30 minutes. Let stand for 30 minutes. Serves 4 to 8. Should be served with boiled potatoes, especially small red potatoes.

MARINATED BEEF CUBES

Phyllis Kelleher

2 lbs. lean round or chuck cut
    in 1" cubes
meat tenderizer
½ C. salad oil
¼ C. vinegar

¼ C. finely chopped onion
1 tsp. salt
1 tsp. coarsely ground pepper
2 tsp. Worcestershire sauce

Tenderize beef as directed in the tenderizer package. In a deep bowl combine all ingredients except meat; mix well. Add meat to marinade and stir to coat. Refrigerate overnight or let stand at room temperature 2 or 3 hours, turning meat occasionally. Place on skewers, and broil over open barbecue until tender. Serves 6.

SWEET & SOUR POT ROAST WITH GINGER SNAP GRAVY

Mildred Nestor

4 lbs. rump roast
salt and pepper
OPTIONAL: garlic
4 T. vegetable oil or fat
¾ - 1 C. cider vinegar
1 - 1½ C. water (or more if needed)

5 - 6 whole cloves
5 - 6 whole allspice
1 tsp. or more pickling spice
1 onion chopped
6 - 7 ginger snaps, grated or whole

Prepare meat by rubbing with salt and pepper, garlic if desired. In a heavy pot, brown on all sides in vegetable oil or fat. When browned, remove from heat. Combine ¾ - 1 C. cider vinegar with 1 - 1½ C. water (add more of each if needed) and pour over meat. Add all the spices plus the chopped onion, and simmer 3 - 3½ hours. When meat is done, remove and set aside.

Strain all of the spices, saving the liquid for gravy. Cool liquid to remove the fat. Put the liquid into a large skillet and add the ginger snaps. Stir thoroughly. Add more water if gravy is too thick. Slice the meat and serve with potato dumplings or potato pancakes. An excellent side dish: red cabbage (prepared).

MEAT LOAF

Rose Kemmett

3 lbs. lean beef chopped
1 egg beaten
½ C. sour cream
½ C. bread crumbs

2 T. dry onion
2 T. dry parsley
pepper and garlic powder to taste

Mix together first 4 ingredients with some water or milk added until you reach consistency you like. Add remaining 3 ingredients, mix into meat mixture, shape into loaf. Bake in oblong baking dish or loaf pan 1 to 1½ hours at 350°.

POT ROAST

Kay Gleeson

2 - 3 lbs. shoulder London broil
1 T. teriyaki
2 - 3 T. oil
3 C. water
1 packet onion soup mix
6 lg. carrots
2 med. tomatoes

1 lg. onion
1 lg. green pepper
4 sticks of celery
4 med. Idaho potatoes, cut in half
Thickener: 2 T. flour - 2 - 3 T. water
Seasoning to taste: salt pepper, garlic
     powder

Marinate meat in teriyaki for 2 hours. In a large skillet brown meat in oil - both sides. Add 3 C. water and onion soup mix. Bring to a boil, reduce heat, cover and simmer for 1½ hours. Cut carrots, tomatoes, onion, green pepper, and celery into small pieces. Add into pot, cover, continue to simmer 30 minutes. Add potatoes, continue to simmer, covered, for another 30 minutes. To thicken gravy: combine flour and 2 - 3 T. water, add to mixture, stir and cook 10 - 15 minutes. Salt, pepper and garlic powder to taste. Serves 6. Serve over noodles.

ULTAN'S SALISBURY STEAKLETS

Louis Ultan

2 lbs. kosher prime chuck steak -
     ground

salt

Form ground steak into four patties of roughly equal size. Sprinkle salt liberally and evenly into aluminum frying pan. Place patties in the pan, turning them frequently to ensure uniform cooking on all sides. When uniformly brown on all sides (deeper brown if desired serving is to be well done), place two patties on each dinner plate. Serve with two vegetables on the same plate. Serves 2.

BEEF IN WINE SAUCE

Maura Dillon Pichetto

2 lbs. beef round, cut in 1½" cubes
bacon grease or
   half butter/half olive oil
1 C. red wine or
   beef broth, or
   ½ red wine - ½ broth
2 carrots, sliced in 2" pieces

2 stalks celery, sliced in 2" pieces
1 lg. onion, cut in quarters
8 oz. tomato sauce
1 bay leaf
½ tsp. oregano
½ tsp. salt; pepper to taste
¾ C. peas

Use a large heavy pan with a cover. Dry beef cubes, brown a few at a time in bacon grease if available, or in half butter/half olive oil. Remove cubes as browned to separate dish. Pour wine or beef broth into pan. Scrape up browned bits in pan. Add browned beef, carrots, celery, onion, tomato sauce, bay leaf, oregano, salt and pepper. Cover. Simmer 1½ - 2 hours until meat is tender. Add additional wine or beef broth if sauce cooks down. Before serving, add peas, simmer 5 minutes or so until peas are cooked. Reheats very well the next day. Serves 6.

BEEF IN BURGUNDY

W. K. Wucherer

¼ C. butter
¼ C. salad oil
1¼ lb. small white onions
2½ T. potato flour, or
   ¼ C. unsifted all-purpose flour
1 tsp. meat extract paste
1 T. tomato paste
4 lbs. chuck, trimmed and
   cut in 2" cubes

¼ tsp. pepper
2 bay leaves
½ tsp. dried thyme leaves
½ tsp. dried marjoram leaf
4 sprigs parsley
¾ lb. mushrooms
chopped parsley
3 C. Burgundy

Preheat oven to 325°. In a 4-qt. Dutch oven, heat butter and oil. Saute onions 5 minutes and remove. Take Dutch oven from heat, discard all but 1 T. of fat. Stir in flour, meat extract paste and tomato paste until smooth. Add beef, pepper, herbs, parsley sprigs and mushrooms, stirring until well mixed. Bake covered 1½ hours. Add onions, bake 1 hour longer, or until meat is tender. Sprinkle with chopped parsley. Gradually add Burgundy, stirring until smooth. Serves 8.

ULTAN'S STEAK STEW

Louis Ultan

2 lbs. kosher chuck steak	1 T. garlic powder
1 lg. onion	1 T. sweet paprika
1 C. water	1 - 8-oz can Del Monte tomato sauce
1 tsp. salt	

Cut steak into roughly 1 - 1½" cubes. Set aside. Peel onion and slice it into a stewpot 8 or 8½" in diameter. Add water, making sure at least 1" is in the pot. Add salt and simmer for 5 minutes. While onion is simmering, season the steak pieces with garlic powder, onion powder and paprika. After onion has simmered, put steak into pot. Simmer for another 5 minutes, then add tomato sauce. Stir. Cover pot and cook for 1 to 1¼ hours, stirring occasionally. Serves 4.

JAEGER SCHNITZEL WITH SPAETZLE

Marie and John
chefs at
Charlie's Inn

6 oz. veal scallopine	¼ C. brown gravy
1 C. flour	6 eggs
1 T. butter	1 C. water
¼ C. mushrooms sliced	¼ tsp. salt
2 T. red wine	flour
2 T. sour cream	

JAEGER SCHNITZEL: Flour veal, saute in butter lightly, brown on each side. Add mushrooms, wine, sour cream, gravy. Bring to slight boil and remove from heat.

SPAETZLE: In a 2-qt. saucepan, bring water to a boil. In a large bowl, mix eggs, add salt, and add flour gradually until mixture becomes dough consistency. With spaetzle-maker or large strainer, lower dough into the boiling water till the pieces rise to top. Strain and cool in cold water. Saute in butter and serve with Jaeger Schnitzel. [Editors' Note: Or visit CHARLIE'S INN, 2711 Harding Avenue.]

BROILED VEAL CHOPS

Francois Tanty - 1906

2 veal chops	½ C. breadcrumbs
½ C. melted butter	OPTIONAL: chopped parsley

Dip chops into the melted butter, roll into the breadcrumbs. Fry them over a low flame until fully cooked and browned. Serve on a warm dish, placing on each chop a little chopped parsley mixed with butter.

VEAL PARMIGIANA BIANCO

Luisa Greco

¾ lb. veal cutlets
1 lb. ricotta cheese
1 lb. dry mozzarella chopped
1 lb. roasted peppers, cut into strips
1 egg
½ C. fresh basil, chopped fine, or
    pesto spread

4 cloves garlic, chopped fine
4 cloves garlic whole
2 T. butter
½ C. white wine
¼ C. olive oil
salt and pepper

Season veal with salt, pepper and chopped garlic. Bake or grill or saute veal -
cook a short time (depending on its thickness). Mix ricotta, mozzarella, egg, two
pinches of basil, salt and pepper. Take undercooked veal, place in a baking pan,
sprinkle some basil or coat with pesto spread. Place small mound of cheese
mixture on each piece of veal (approx. 2 T.), then cross with strips of red
peppers. Bake 10 minutes.

SAUCE: Saute garlic in olive oil. When garlic is browned, add remainder of red
peppers and butter, saute 5 minutes. Add majority of basil and the white wine
and simmer a few minutes. Place oven-baked veal in serving dish and pour
sauce. Garnish with remainder of basil.

STUFFED BREAST OF VEAL - ROASTED

Lillian Schwartz

1 breast of veal (with pocket)
½ lb. onions, chopped
4 cloves garlic, crushed
vegetable oil for frying
1 carrot, grated

¼ C. cream of rice (uncooked) or farina
½ box crushed cornflakes (sm. single
    serving box)
2 eggs beaten
salt, pepper, paprika to taste

Fry onions and garlic in oil. Grate carrot. Mix everything together and stuff in
pocket of veal breast. Season top of veal breast with salt, pepper and paprika
and brush top with oil lightly. Roast, covered, in preheated oven at 325° for
2½ hours. Last 15 minutes raise heat to 450° to brown on top. Serves 6.

FRIED TRIPE

Charles Vogeler Company - c.1880s

2 lbs. tripe
1 T. oil
2 T. vinegar

salt and pepper
1 C. flour or 1 C. breadcrumbs

Boil tripe until soft; remove from heat and cool. Cut cold boiled tripe into pieces 3" square and lay them for ½ hour in a mixture of oil, vinegar, salt and pepper. Roll the pieces of tripe in salted flour (or breadcrumbs) and fry in oil. Drain off the excess oil and serve.

BRAISED HOT PEPPER PORK CHOPS

Peter Derrick

6 center cut pork chops,
  cut 1½" thick
1 lg. white onion, sliced
2 cloves garlic, chopped
3 T. olive oil
2 T. flour
garlic salt and pepper
1 cup dry white wine

½ C. sweet rice wine
  (or cooking sherry)
½ C. water
3 T. Korean hot pepper bean paste (ko chu chang) or 2 T. Chinese hot chile paste
2 C. sauerkraut, with juice

In a large frying pan, that has a lid, saute the onion and garlic in 1 T. olive oil for 3 minutes. Remove and set aside. Lightly dust the pork chops in flour, shaking off the excess. Sprinkle chops with garlic salt and pepper. Brown the chops in frying pan in 2 T. olive oil over medium high heat for 2-3 minutes on each side. Set aside and clean pan. In pan, mix wine, sweet wine, water and Korean hot pepper paste and warm. Add pork chops and onion/garlic mix. Add 2 C. sauerkraut, with juice. Bring to a boil. Cover pan with lid, lower heat and simmer over low heat for 1¼ hours.

Serve pork chops with sauerkraut on top, with white rice on the side. Use pan juice as gravy. Serves 6 (or 3 big eaters).

ORANGE FLAVORED PORK

Ina B. Greiner

5 - 6 lb. fresh pork shoulder
1 C. water
1 lg. onion
2 - 3 bay leaves

2 - 3 peppercorns
salt
1 C. orange juice

Rinse meat in cold water. Place in a pressure cooker with water, onion, bay leaves, salt and peppercorns. Cook 15 minutes per pound or until meat begins to fall away from the bone. Remove the skin and fat. Shred meat and place in shallow baking pan. Cover with orange juice and bake in a 350° oven for 20 minutes. Thoroughly mix meat and liquid in pan. Serve over rice.

NOTE: Skin can be cut into pieces, seasoned to taste, and cooked in the oven until crisp. This makes a delicious snack.

PORK CHOPS AND POTATOES - STEAMED

Ann Revi

4 - 6 pork or lamb chops - lg. bones
    removed
mixture of herbed breadcrumbs, flour,
    paprika

cooking oil
2 - 4 cloves of garlic
3 - 4 potatoes, peeled
salt and pepper

Wash the chops and pat dry. Coat them with herbed breadcrumbs, flour and paprika mixture. Saute chops in small amount of oil until brown on both sides. Add garlic and brown.

Slice potatoes ¼" thick. Use large pan with cover. Cover bottom of pan with sliced potatoes, placing smaller ends against side of pan. Place meat and garlic on top and cover with lid. Place on low heat and let steam for 15 minutes, or until potatoes are done. Season with salt and pepper. Serve potatoes browned side up. Discard garlic. Pan gravy can be made by adding cup of water to pan. Bring to boil and simmer a few minutes.

DEVILED HAM

Charles Vogeler Company - c.1880s

2 thick slices smoked ham
½ tsp. mustard
dash of cayenne pepper

½ tsp. tart jelly
3 T. vinegar
1 T. sherry

Fry ham in a pan until the edges begin to crisp. Transfer to a dish and keep hot. Into the fat left in the pan stir in the mustard, dash of cayenne pepper, jelly and vinegar. Bring to a quick boil, add a great spoonful of sherry and pour over the ham. Serve hot.

CHICKEN BREASTS WITH MOZZARELLA

Karlan Sick

PER PERSON:
One boneless chicken breast
1 slice mozzarella

1 slice prosciutto
sm. glass white wine
pepper

Saute 1 boneless chicken breast per person for approx. 3 minutes on the first side. Turn over. Season with fresh ground pepper or red pepper to taste. Place a slice of prosciutto on each and top with a slice of mozzarella. Pour a small glass of white wine in pan and cover pan until cheese melts. VARIATION: Omit prosciutto and sprinkle with capers.

BROILED CHICKEN (DEVILED)

Allen Slatky

1 whole chicken
1 T. butter
½ tsp. mustard

1 tsp. vinegar
pinch of cayenne
breadcrumbs

Clean chicken, split down the back. Broil until done and starting to brown. Lay chicken in a pan and rub all over with a sauce made by whipping together the butter, mustard, vinegar and cayenne (save some sauce for later). Sift the breadcrumbs over all and put back into the oven until brown. Transfer to a hot dish and pour sauce over chicken.

CHICKEN AND MUSHROOMS BENNETT

Chef Rodneey DiBenedetto

1 whole chicken
all-purpose flour
1 T. basil to taste
¼ T. pepper to taste
butter (or margarine)
olive oil
2 C. fresh mushrooms, sliced

3 cloves garlic, chopped fine
2½ T. parsley chopped
3 - 4 bay leaves
chicken stock (broth)
oregano, basil to taste
salt and pepper to taste

Cut and quarter 1 chicken (medium to large). Mix 1½ C. flour with approx. 1 T. basil and ¼ T. pepper to taste. Flour chicken and refrigerate approximately 20 minutes or until doughy, then reflour. In a large skillet or fry pan (with lid) saute chicken in butter and oil (enough to coat), cook until brown, then remove chicken. In the same pan saute 2 cups fresh sliced mushrooms, 3 cloves garlic chopped fine, and about 2½ T. parsley chopped, and then put chicken back in pan. Add bay leaves (3 - 4), 2 cups of chicken stock, cover and simmer 20 minutes stirring occasionally, and add ½ cup more stock and salt to taste. Cook for 30 to 40 minutes or until soup absorbs into a sauce, stirring every 15 minutes. Towards the end stir more frequently to prevent sticking. Keep on a low flame. Cooking time may vary according to the size of the chicken. OPTIONAL: Serve on a bed of white rice or egg noodles.

CHICKEN CREOLE

Stacey Hogarty

1 lbs. cubed chicken cutlet
1 sm. onion cut in rings
2 T. oil
1 lg. can whole tomatoes

3 cloves garlic, crushed
4 bay leaves
OPTIONAL: cayenne pepper

In a large pan saute onions in oil. Add cubed chicken. Cook till chicken is white. Add whole tomatoes. Gently mash whole tomatoes while cooking. Add garlic, bay leaves and cayenne pepper if desired. Simmer for 45 minutes stirring occasionally. Remove bay leaves before serving. Serve over cooked rice.

CHICKEN FLORENTINE

Ronnie Greenberg

2 pkgs. frozen spinach, cooked
5 chicken breasts, boned, skinned and split
melted butter

flour
1½ C. whipping cream
paprika
Parmesan cheese

Put cooked spinach in bottom of casserole. Dredge breasts in melted butter and flour and fry till brown. Place on top of spinach and pour whipping cream over it. Sprinkle with paprika and Parmesan cheese. Bake 20 minutes at 400°.

EVA'S LEMON CHICKEN

Lucy Greenstein

1 - 3 lb. chicken cut in ⅛s
2 T. grated lemon peel
½ C. lemon juice
2 cloves garlic crushed

2 tsp. thyme
1 tsp. salt
1 tsp. pepper
¼ C. butter, melted

Arrange chicken in single layer in shallow pan. Combine lemon peel, juice, garlic, thyme, salt and pepper. Mix well and spoon over chicken. Refrigerate 3 - 4 hours. Preheat oven at 425°. Brush melted butter over chicken. Bake uncovered 25 minutes. Turn chicken, bake 25 - 30 minutes more until chicken is browned.

CHICKEN-N-STUFFING SCALLOP

Audrey Noonan

1 (8 oz.) pkg. herb-seasoned stuffing mix
3 C. cubed cooked chicken or turkey
½ C. butter or margarine
½ C. enriched flour

¼ tsp. salt
dash pepper
4 C. chicken broth
6 eggs slightly beaten

Prepare stuffing according to package directions. Spread in 9×13×2" pan. Top with a layer of chicken (or turkey).

In a large pot, melt butter (or margarine), blend in flour and seasonings, add cool broth, cook and stir until thickened. Stir small amount of hot mixture into eggs, return to hot mixture, pour over chicken. Bake in slow oven 325° for 40 - 45 minutes until knife inserted in center comes out clean. Let stand 5 minutes to set.

OOO LA LA CHICKEN

Elizabeth J. Hall

1 whole chicken or equal
½ stick of butter or margarine (4 T.)
¼ C. Wondra flour
1 lg. yellow onion, sliced

cooking or dry sherry
salt and pepper (white) and other
seasonings to taste

Prepare chicken, cut in pieces, or equivalent amount of pieces, for cooking, best skinned. In a large skillet (with lid), place butter (or margarine). Add chicken and brown. As each piece is turned, sprinkle with flour. When flouring second side of chicken, allow some flour to fall into the melted butter in the skillet. Arrange in one layer and place sliced onion in a single layer. Dilute sherry with boiling water in a one-to-three (1:3) mixture and almost cover chicken with same. Lower heat, cover pan, and simmer till done over low heat, about 45 minutes. Serve with rice. Gravy produced in the pan is excellent.

CHICKEN ASPARAGUS PINWHEELS

Dave Greco

¾ lb. chicken (or veal) cutlets, pounded
   out*
6 oz. prosciutto, sliced
8 oz. dry mozzarella
4 cloves garlic chopped
   parsley
1 lb. steamed asparagus

¼ C. olive oil
4 cloves garlic whole
SAUCE: Previous ingredients and:
½ C. chicken broth
4 lemons, 2 for juice, 2 for wedges
¼ C. white wine
salt and pepper

* Veal cutlets may be substituted. To pound out cutlets, place separately between waxed paper and pound with mallet.

Place over each cutlet 1 slice prosciutto and dry mozzarella, then sprinkle with chopped garlic and parsley, and lay asparagus lengthwise over this (leave some asparagus for the sauce). Roll cutlets (with contents) and seal with toothpicks. Make sure no contents are exposed. Saute the rolled cutlets in olive oil and garlic until lightly browned and tender. -Or- Place rolled cutlets on coated cookie sheet, bake at 375° for 10 to 15 minutes, depending on thickness of cutlets.

SAUCE: Saute olive oil and garlic. Add remaining pieces of asparagus (cut in 2" pieces), chicken broth, juice of two lemons, and remaining ingredients. Let simmer approximately 10 minutes. Place rolls in decorative dish, pour sauce over them, garnish with parsley and lemon wedges.

HELEN PLACKO'S CHICKEN VEGETABLE STEW

Mary T. Placko

1 broiler/fryer (2½ to 3 lbs.), cut up
4½ C. water
2 tsp. salt
2 (8 oz.) cans tomato sauce
2 med. onions, quartered
4 carrots, pared and cut into 2"
    pieces
3 stalks celery with tops, sliced
diagonally
½ C. fresh parsley
1 bay leaf
1 can (8 oz.) whole kernel corn,
    drained
2½ T. flour (or cornstarch)
5½ tsp. water
Hot cooked rice (or noodles)

Place chicken, water and salt in kettle with tight-fitting cover. Simmer covered for one hour. Remove chicken and skim fat from broth. Stir in tomato sauce, onions, carrots, celery, parsley and bay leaf. Cover, simmer 20 to 25 minutes, or until vegetables are tender. Remove bay leaf.

Meanwhile, remove skin and bones from chicken, leaving meat in large pieces. Add to broth along with corn when vegetables are tender. Remove from heat. Make a smooth paste of the flour (or cornstarch) and water and stir into stew. Simmer, uncovered, 3 minutes. Serve stew in deep soup bowls. Top each portion with scoop of hot cooked rice (or noodles).

JAMAICAN CURRIED GOAT (OR LAMB)

Marjorie Ford

1 lb. boneless goat meat (or lamb), cut in 1" cubes
2 T. vegetable oil
2 large onions, finely sliced
2 tsp. allspice
2 C. stock (or beef consomme or
    bouillon)
1 T. wine vinegar
1 tsp. curry powder
salt and cayenne pepper to taste
½ bay leaf
½ tsp. Tabasco sauce

Brown meat in oil in large frying pan, that has a lid, for 4-5 minutes. Remove meat from pan. Saute onion in pan until soft, but not brown. Stir in curry powder and allspice. Cook for one minute and then stir in stock, wine vinegar, salt and cayenne pepper. Return meat to pan, cover pan and simmer over low heat for 2 hours. Add bay leaf 30 minutes before completion. Stir in Tabasco sauce at end. Serve with white rice. Serves 4.

STUFFED CHICKEN JUNE

Paul Eisland

2 whole chicken breasts split and butter-flied (your butcher can do it for you), pounded flat

2 T. oil (olive or canola)
1 C. chicken stock
THE STUFFING
½ med. onion chopped (about ½ C.)
1 stalk celery diced
3 med. mushrooms diced
salt and pepper to taste

1 tsp. assorted herbs, your choice (parsley, oregano, thyme)
½ C. breadcrumbs
½ C. sweet vermouth
2 T. oil (olive or canola ... butter if you dare)

Saute the onions, celery and mushrooms in the oil over medium heat until translucent and tender, add herbs and salt and pepper and transfer to bowl. Add breadcrumbs and mix well. Add up to ¼ cup vermouth to moisten the stuffing mix.

Place flattened chicken breast on a piece of plastic wrap. Put 1½ to 2 T. stuffing mix in center of chicken breast along the longest side and fold over the ends to keep in stuffing and roll using the wrap to help form a tight roll. (Be sure to remove plastic wrap from rolls before cooking.) Use toothpicks to secure the ends. Make four rolls the same way. Heat oven to 350°. Add oil to a skillet with an ovenproof handle (skillet should be large enough to hold all four stuffed breasts) over medium heat and brown chicken on all sides (3 - 4 minutes).

When brown, remove from stove and add chicken stock to pan. Place in oven and cook for 20 minutes, basting with pan juices after 10 minutes.

Remove from oven, transfer to cutting surface. Cover and allow to rest. Deglaze pan with balance of vermouth and reduce until sauce begins to thicken slightly. Slice each roll into ¾ to 1" pieces, arrange on individual plate and spoon sauce over chicken. Serve with rice or grain and something green. Serves 4.

BRONX DUCK

Peter Derrick

1 duck (defrosted if frozen)
1 C. Saucy Susan sauce (or
sweet and sour sauce)
½ C. Korean hot pepper bean
paste (ko chu chang)
   or 2 T. Chinese hot chili
paste (or 1 oz. Tabasco

sauce as a last resort)
1 oz. soy sauce
pinch garlic salt
pinch black pepper
1 orange
1 oz. Grand Marnier or
   Triple Sec (orange liqueur)

Preheat oven to 450°. Wash out inside of duck. Punch holes in skin of duck
with tip of sharp knife (to allow fat to escape in first ½ hour of cooking).
Sprinkle inside and outside of duck with garlic salt and black pepper. Cut
orange in half and place halves inside duck cavity. Place duck on rack in
roasting pan. Cook in oven on high heat (450°) for ½ hour to let fat melt. Take
duck from oven and put on platter. Drain fat from roasting pan. Return duck to
rack in pan and replace in oven. Reduce heat to 350° and cook for 1½ hours.

Combine Saucy Susan sauce, Korean red pepper paste (or substitute) and soy
sauce in bowl. Take duck out of oven (after it has cooked for the 1½ hours)
and baste it with half of the sauce (which will form a glaze in the oven).
Return duck to 350° oven for 15 - 20 minutes (do not let glaze burn).

Remove duck from the oven and put on a large platter. Pour orange liqueur over
the duck. Light the liqueur with a match and let the fire burn until it goes out.
Remove orange from cavity. Let duck sit for 10 minutes before carving. Carve
into 6 to 8 pieces. Use remaining sauce to dip duck in. Serve with white rice.
Serves 3 or 4.

FISH, PAN FRIED

Dave Neary

2 lbs. fresh or frozen fish fillets
1 egg, beaten
2 T. water

¼ C. cornmeal
oil or shortening
seasoning to taste

Cut fillets into portions. Combine egg and water. Mix cornmeal, salt, and
pepper. Dip fish into egg mixture, then into cornmeal mixture. Fry over medium
heat till brown, 4 to 5 minutes each side. Drain off oil.

FISH AND CHIPS

Michael Boyd

1 lb. fish fillets	1 T. cooking oil
3 baking potatoes, peeled	1 egg yolk
oil for frying	1 beaten egg white
¼ C. all-purpose flour	¼ C. all-purpose flour
½ tsp. salt	salt
2 T. water	malt vinegar

Cut fish into serving-size pieces. Pat dry with paper towel. Cut potatoes in uniform strips slightly larger than French fries. Fry a few at a time in deep hot oil (375°) till golden. In a bowl, stir together ¼ C. flour and ½ tsp. salt. Add water, oil, and egg yolk, beat smooth. Fold in beaten egg white.

Dip fish in ¼ C. flour and then in batter. Fry fish in deep hot oil (350°) till golden brown, 1½ to 2 minutes on each side. To serve, season fish and chips with salt and drizzle with malt vinegar. Serves 4.

FISH IN WINE SAUCE

Geri Olbermann

2 lbs. flounder or other fillets	⅓ C. dry white wine
3 tomatoes, sliced	½ tsp. basil
2 T. flour	plain breadcrumbs
2 T. melted butter	parsley, chopped
½ C. skim or buttermilk	

Place fillets in a single layer in baking dish. Arrange sliced tomatoes over top of fillets. Blend flour into butter in saucepan. Add milk gradually and cook till thickened, stirring constantly. Remove from heat and stir in wine and basil. Pour sauce over top of tomatoes and fish, add crumbs. Bake at 350° until fish flakes easily when tested with fork. Sprinkle with parsley before serving.

BLUEFISH DELIGHT

Dimitri Menedev

bluefish fillets, 6 - 8 oz. per portion
1 clove garlic chopped, or 1 tsp. garlic
    powder
½ C. white wine
6 T. olive oil

3 scallions chopped
1 C. breadcrumbs
1 egg
¼ tsp. pepper
salt if desired

Beat egg and coat fillets on both sides. Coat with breadcrumbs. Place fillets into olive oil in a heavy pan and cook 5 minutes or so and then add the wine, garlic powder, scallions, pepper and salt (if desired), and cook until fish is flaky.

POACHED CODFISH STEAK

Kay Gleeson

2 codfish steaks
1 sm. onion
¼ C. milk

2 T. butter
2 slices lemon

In frying pan, saute finely chopped onion in melted butter until moist, not brown. Add milk. Add codfish steaks. Top each with lemon slice. Salt and pepper to taste. Cover - simmer over very low heat for 30 minutes. Serves 2. Serve with cauliflower and bread.

STEWED EELS, ENGLISH STYLE

Charles Vogeler Company · c.1880s

4 lbs. of eels
1 C. veal or chicken broth
1 T. minced onion
2 T. butter
salt and pepper

1 T. minced parsley
2 eggs
juice of one lemon
1 C. sherry or white wine

Cut eels in pieces 2" long and put in skillet with the broth and onion. Cook till tender, add the butter and seasoning. Cover closely and simmer for 10 minutes. Remove the eels and keep hot in dish. Add to the gravy in skillet: parsley, two eggs beaten carefully, then the lemon juice and wine. Bring to boil and at once pour over eels.

SOFT SHELL CRABS

Charles Vogeler Company - c.1880s

soft shell crabs
2 eggs, beaten
2 C. breadcrumbs

oil
lemons
cayenne pepper

Pull off spongy parts on backs, under the sides of the shells, and from the lower side of the body. Wash and wipe the crabs, dip in raw beaten egg, then in fine crumbs, and fry in oil about 10 minutes. Drain off the oil, lay crabmeat on a heated platter. Garnish with parsley and cayenne pepper. Serve with lemons cut into eighths.

BROILED LOBSTER

Peg O'Connor

1 whole lobster
2 T. olive oil
salt and pepper to taste

parsley for garnish
OPTIONAL: tartar sauce

Cut lobster in two, lengthwise; place halves on an ovenproof dish. Pour over it the olive oil, salt and pepper, and broil on moderate flame for about 20 minutes, turning from time to time. Serve with parsley garnish and tartar sauce.

BROILED SHRIMP WITH GARLIC

Veronica Stewart

2 lbs. shrimp, shelled
¾ C. butter
⅓ C. olive oil
⅔ C. chopped onions
1½ T. minced garlic

3 - 4 T. freshly squeezed lime juice
pinch cayenne pepper
⅓ C. minced parsley
salt to taste

Preheat broiler to 550°. Heat butter and olive oil together in a large ovenproof pan. Add onions and garlic and slowly cook them for about 5 minutes or until softened but not browned. Stir in lime juice, cayenne pepper and shrimp. Continue stirring until the shrimp are coated with the butter mixture. Sprinkle with minced parsley and broil shrimp for 5 - 7 minutes, basting once or twice.

COCONUT-BEER SHRIMP

Tina Walker

1 lb. shrimp, shelled and deveined,
    leaving tails on
1 tsp. salt
1 tsp. black pepper
½ tsp. garlic powder
½ tsp. onion powder
½ tsp. ground thyme
½ tsp. ground oregano
¾ C. flour
¼ C. beer

1 egg beaten
½ tsp. baking powder
1 pkg. coconut oil for frying

ORANGE SAUCE:
1 jar orange marmalade
2 T. horseradish
3 T. spicy brown mustard
½ tsp. lemon rind, grated

Make orange sauce: in a bowl combine marmalade, horseradish, mustard and lemon rind. Chill. In a separate bowl combine all spices; mix well and set aside. In a medium bowl, combine flour, beer, egg and baking powder. Mix well. Dip shrimp first into seasonings mixture, shaking off excess. Then dip seasoned shrimp into batter. Dredge batter-coated shrimp in coconut. Fry shrimp, 5 or 6 at a time, in deep 350° oil, for 45 seconds on each side or until golden brown. Drain on paper towels. Serve with orange sauce.

SHRIMP CANTONESE

Margaret Chu

1 lb. shrimp
¼ lb. ground pork
¼ C. peanut oil
2 tsp. minced garlic
1 T. salted black beans
½ tsp. salt
2 - 3 T. chicken broth

5 slices quarter-size fresh ginger roots
¼ tsp. sesame oil
¼ tsp. thin soy sauce
3 stalks of scallions, diced
1 tsp. tapioca powder dissolved in 1 T.
    water
1 egg, beaten

1. Shell shrimp and devein. Wash and pat dry.
2. Heat wok, add peanut oil. Stir-fry garlic and black beans.
3. Add pork, stir-fry until color changes.
4. Add shrimp and salt. Stir-fry until just done or when pink color appears.
5. Add chicken broth and ginger. Stir-fry and bring to boiling point.
6. Add sesame oil, thin soy sauce, scallions and tapioca mixture
7. When sauce begins to bubble again, add egg and stir-fry.
8. Remove from wok. Serve hot.

NOTES

22621B-ca

CAKES & COOKIES,
JAMS & PRESERVES, DESSERTS

Zephyrs
Apple Dump Cake
Pineapple Cake
Jewish Apple Cake
Whiskey Cake
Cheesecake
Black Walnut Cookies
Mandelbread
Ricotta Cookies
Sugar Monster Cookies
Blueberry Muffins
Walnut Apricot Shortbread
Best Ever Coffee Cake
Grandma Pearl Blueberry Muffins
Delicious Brownies
Pumpkin Muffins
Hot Golden Fruit Compote
Grape Nut Pudding
Strawberry Jello Mold

Old Fashioned Bread Pudding
Charlotte Russe
Chocolate Mousse
Eggo Waffle Dessert/Snack
Pecan Pie
Chocolate Truffles
Peanut Butter Ice Cream Pie
Rice Pudding
Hamantashen
Fruit Pudding
Strawberry-Rhubarb Pie
Party Pecan Tarts
Biscuit Rings
Mom's Applesauce
Banana Jam
Lime Marmalade
Peach Preserves
Bronx Mulberry Jam
Red Pepper Jam

ZEPHYRS

Phyllis Festa Podlaski

¾ C. unsalted butter, softened
½ C. sugar
2 tsp. real vanilla extract
1 lg. egg

2 C. all-purpose flour
½ tsp. salt
½ C. walnuts finely chopped
6 oz. semisweet chocolate pieces

Heat oven to 350°. Cream butter and sugar together until fluffy. Stir in vanilla. Add egg and beat thoroughly. Sift flour and salt together or shake through a strainer into the egg and butter mixture. Add nuts and chocolate. Shape into balls 1½" in diameter. Bake 15 minutes. Makes 4 dozen.

APPLE DUMP CAKE

Eve Curci

1 can Comstock apples
2 eggs
1 tsp. cinnamon
¾ C. oil
1 tsp. vanilla
1½ C. sugar, or if diabetic, substitute 6 - 7 packets Sweet & Low instead

1 C. coarsely chopped walnuts
1 tsp. salt
2 C. flour
1 tsp. baking soda

Stir all ingredients well with a spoon (no electric mixer) in a bowl, pour into a greased 9×13" baking pan. Bake 1 hour at 350°. Cool, then remove from pan.

PINEAPPLE CAKE

Audrey Noonan

1 pkg. yellow cake mix
1 can (15-oz.) crushed pineapple (do not drain)
1 C. sugar

1 pkg. (6 oz.) instant vanilla pudding
1 lg. Cool Whip
2 bananas
toasted coconut (optional)

Bake yellow cake mix as directed in 9×13" pan. Let cool and then poke holes in cake with wooden spoon handle. In saucepan, heat pineapple and sugar until sugar dissolves. Pour over cake. Slice bananas and top cake with them. Mix instant pudding with 2 C. of milk, pour over cake. Put Cool Whip on top and sprinkle with toasted coconut if desired.

JEWISH APPLE CAKE

Mary T. Placko

4 C. flour
2 C. sugar
½ tsp. salt
4 tsp. baking powder
1 C. orange juice
1 C. salad oil

4 eggs
5 - 6 apples, peeled, cored and sliced
CINNAMON/SUGAR Mix:
2 T. cinnamon
1 C. granulated sugar

OPTIONAL: ½ - ¾ C. chopped walnuts or pecans added to batter, in the middle and on top

Sift flour, sugar, salt and baking powder together. Make a well in the center of mixture, stir in the orange juice, salad oil and eggs and beat well. Pour half of this mixture into a greased 10" tube pan, add half of the sliced apples (and optional nuts) on top of the batter. Sprinkle with the cinnamon/sugar mix, then add the rest of the batter, put remainder of apples on the top, and again sprinkle with more "Mix" (nuts optional on top). Bake in a 350° oven approx. 2 hours, or until tested with knife inserted into center comes out clean. Enjoy the delicious aroma while the cake bakes, as well as the taste when done!

WHISKEY CAKE

Naomi Schildwachter Herron

1 box yellow cake mix
1 box instant vanilla pudding
4 eggs
½ C. oil
½ C. milk

½ C. water
1 C. butter
½ C. whiskey
½ C. sugar

Mix the first six ingredients together and bake in angel food pan at 350° for 1 hour or until done. Melt 1 C. butter, ½ C. whiskey, and ½ C. sugar in small pan until bubbly. Pour over cake and bake 5 minutes more. This cake freezes well. If desired, confectioners sugar can be sprinkled.

CHEESECAKE

Frances La Bollita

4 (8-oz.) pkgs. of cream cheese
1 lb. sour cream
1 stick butter
1 C. sugar
3 eggs

3 T. cornstarch
3 T. flour
1½ T. vanilla
1½ T. lemon juice
OPTIONAL: 1 can of cherries or 1 can blueberries*

Preheat oven to 350°. Grease and flour a 9" spring pan. Soften cream cheese and cream it, fold in sour cream. Melt butter and blend in. Fold in sugar a little at a time. Add eggs 1 at a time. Add flour 1 T. at a time. Add cornstarch 1 T. at a time. Finally add vanilla and lemon. Bake in preheated 350° oven for 1 hour, do not open door. Turn off oven after 1 hour and leave in undisturbed for 1 more hour. Should be light golden brown. Remove from oven and let cool to room temperature. Loosen spring pan easily, remove side of pan. Put dish on top of cheesecake and carefully turn over.

*You could either put the cherries or blueberries on top of the cake or in a dish to use when ready on individual pieces, according to preferences.

BLACK WALNUT COOKIES

Jill Rosenfeld

3 sticks unsalted butter, softened
¾ C. granulated sugar
3 eggs
2 C. unbleached all-purpose flour

¼ tsp. salt
1 tsp. vanilla extract
⅔ C. shelled black walnuts, finely chopped

In a bowl of an electric mixer, cream butter and sugar until light and fluffy. Mix in eggs, one at a time, beating well after each addition; add vanilla.

In another bowl, sift together the flour with the salt and add to the creamed mixture. Mix well. Wrap dough in plastic wrap and refrigerate for 4 to 6 hours. When thoroughly chilled, roll out to ⅜" thickness, and cut with a cookie cutter 1" in diameter. Place 1½" apart on ungreased baking sheets. Sprinkle cookies with black walnuts and chill again for 45 minutes. Preheat oven to 325°. Bake for 15 minutes, or until cookies are evenly and lightly browned. Remove from sheets and cool on a rack. Makes 5 dozen cookies.

MANDELBREAD

Diane Steinberg

¼ C. butter
¾ C. sugar
2 eggs
2 C. flour

1 tsp. baking powder
1 tsp. vanilla
nuts and fruit

Grease and flour a bread pan. Mix all ingredients and roll into loaf. Bake at 350° for 35 minutes. Remove from oven. Cool slightly. Cut, at a bit of an angle, into ½ to ¾" slices. Cool on wire rack. Store in tight container. Can be kept 2 - 3 weeks.

RICOTTA COOKIES

Phyllis Carile

¼ lb. butter
½ C. ricotta
1 tsp. vanilla
1 C. sugar

1 egg
2 C. flour
½ tsp. baking soda
½ tsp. salt

Preheat oven to 350°. Soften butter, blend with ricotta until creamy. Add vanilla and mix well. Add sugar gradually. Add egg and mix well. Add baking soda, salt and 1 C. flour and stir slowly. Stir in last cup of flour and stir well. Place teaspoon drops on cookie sheet, greased. Bake approximately 15 minutes.

SUGAR MONSTER COOKIES

Dolores Lessner

½ C. shortening
1 C. sugar
½ C. plain yogurt - room temp.
1 egg
2¾ C. all-purpose flour

1½ tsp. baking powder
1 tsp. baking soda
½ tsp. salt
1 tsp. vanilla extract
about 1 T. sugar

Preheat oven to 350°. Generously grease 2 large baking sheets. Cream shortening in a large bowl. Add 1 C. sugar and beat till fluffy. Add egg, mix well. Stir yogurt until creamy. Blend yogurt into creamed mixture. Combine flour, baking powder, baking soda and salt, and vanilla extract, then stir in. Drop by tsp. onto prepared baking sheets. Dip the bottom of a custard cup in 1 T. sugar and press cookies to flatten. Dip custard cup in sugar for each cookie. Bake 10 - 12 minutes until lightly browned. Cool on wire racks. Yield: 24 cookies.

BLUEBERRY MUFFINS

Connie Persichina

2 C. flour
1½ tsp. baking powder
¼ tsp. salt
½ C. butter
1 C. sugar

2 eggs
1 tsp. vanilla
½ C. milk
1 C. blueberries

In a large bowl, at high speed mix butter, sugar and eggs until fluffy. At low speed, add ¼ C. flour and ¼ C. milk, then add rest of flour and milk gradually. Wash berries and fold in. Put mixture into muffin tin and bake at 350° for 20 - 25 minutes. Have a cup of coffee with a friend and enjoy!

WALNUT APRICOT SHORTBREAD

Maura Dillon Pichetto

STEP 1
1 C. sifted flour
⅓ C. sugar
1 stick butter (soft, cut in pieces)
STEP 2
1 C. dried apricots, cut in quarters

2 lg. eggs
1 C. dark brown sugar
⅓ C. flour
½ tsp. baking powder
¼ tsp. salt
1 C. walnut pieces

STEP 1: Combine three ingredients until mixture is in little bits. Line 8" square pain with foil, including up sides (will help with removal). Press mixture into bottom of pan, about ⅓" thick. Bake at 350° for 30 - 40 minutes. It should be a pale tan color. Set aside.
STEP 2: Cook cut apricots in ¾ cup water until soft. Drain out on paper towel, set aside to dry a little. Very lightly beat 2 eggs, add brown sugar, mix well. Combine flour, baking powder and salt. Add to brown sugar/egg mixture. Add apricot and walnut pieces. Pour over cake in pan. Bake at 350° in middle of oven for 40 - 45 minutes. Let cool on rack. Remove from pan, using foil to help, and cut in strips or squares.

BEST EVER COFFEE CAKE

Patricia Walsh

3 C. sifted flour
3 tsp. baking powder
1 tsp. salt
1 C. soft shortening
1 C. sugar
2 eggs, unbeaten
1 C. milk

1½ C. coarsely chopped walnuts
1½ C. light brown sugar, packed
3 T. flour
3 T. cinnamon
¾ C. melted butter
1½ C. raisins, rinsed in hot water
1 tsp. vanilla

Preheat oven to 350°. Grease bottom of one 10×13×2" or two 9×9" pans. Sift the first three ingredients. Mix thoroughly shortening with sugar, then add eggs and beat until very light and fluffy. Beat in alternately flour mixture in fourths and milk and vanilla in thirds. Spread half of batter in pan. Top with half of combined brown sugar, flour and cinnamon. Pour on half of melted butter, then sprinkle half the raisins and nuts. Repeat. Bake at 350° for 50 minutes or until done.

GRANDMA PEARL BLUEBERRY MUFFINS

Lucy Greenstein

½ stick of butter, softened
¾ C. sugar
1½ tsp. baking powder
pinch of baking soda
1 C. blueberries

1 egg
1½ C. flour
½ tsp. salt
½ C. milk
½ tsp. vanilla

Preheat oven 400°. Grease or line with paper cups - muffin tins for 12 muffins. In a large bowl cream butter and sugar. Add egg. Mix well. Sift flour, baking powder and salt into a small bowl. Add flour mixture and milk alternately to butter mixture. Coat blueberries with 1 T. flour and fold into batter. Fill tins ¾ full and bake 20 minutes.

DELICIOUS BROWNIES

Frances La Bollita

2 C. all-purpose flour
2 C. granulated sugar
½ C. (1 stick) butter or margarine
½ C. shortening
1 C. strong brewed coffee or water
¼ C. dark, unsweetened cocoa
½ C. buttermilk*
2 eggs
1 tsp. baking soda
1 tsp. vanilla

FROSTING
½ C. (1 stick) butter or margarine.
2 T. dark cocoa
¼ C. milk
3½ C. unsifted powdered sugar
1 tsp. vanilla

*If you do not have buttermilk on hand, substitute 2 tsp. vinegar or lemon juice mixed into ½ C. whole milk.

In a large mixing bowl, combine the flour and sugar. In a heavy saucepan, combine butter, shortening, coffee (or water) and cocoa. Stir and heat to boiling. Pour boiling mixture over the flour and sugar in the bowl. Add the buttermilk, eggs, baking soda and vanilla. Mix well, using a wooden spoon or high-speed electric mixer. Pour into a 11×17½" baking pan, greased well with butter, and bake at 400° for 20 minutes or until brownies test done in center.

While brownies bake, prepare the frosting. In a saucepan, combine the butter, cocoa and milk. Heat to boiling, stirring. Mix in the powdered sugar and vanilla until frosting is smooth. Pour the warm frosting over the brownies as soon as you take them out of the oven. Cut into 48 bars.

PUMPKIN MUFFINS

Leslie Ann Hogan

DRY: 1¼ C. rye flour (or 1 C. rye and ¼ C. other flour, e.g., oat, millet, quinoa, soy or buckwheat)

2 T. oat bran

½ - 1 tsp. salt

½ tsp. baking powder

½ tsp. baking soda

1 tsp. ground cinnamon

½ tsp. ground nutmeg

¼ tsp. ground cloves

LIQUID:

2 eggs beaten

½ C. vegetable oil (canola or safflower)

½ C. cooked and pureed carrots

1 C. pureed pumpkin

1 tsp. vanilla extract

Preheat oven to 350°. Oil and flour 12 cup muffin tin, or place 12 muffin cups in 12 cup muffin tin. (I use paper muffin cups.) In large bowl combine dry ingredients. In a smaller bowl combine eggs, oil, carrots, vanilla and pumpkin.

Add liquid mixture to dry ingredients and stir until just mixed. (You can also add raisins, currants, chopped walnuts or chopped pecans to vary texture and taste. Experiment!) Spoon mixture into muffin cups. Bake for 25 minutes or until toothpick inserted into center of one large muffin comes out clean. Muffins do not brown on top. Let cool on wire rack. Cool completely if using paper muffin cups to prevent crumbling when removing paper. Refrigerate to keep for 2 - 3 days if they aren't all eaten immediately. Makes 12 muffins.

NOTE: These are delicious sweet breakfast muffins for those on anti-Candida diet, or those with food allergies to wheat, corn, sugar or yeast The muffins are a delicious breakfast treat or a sweet dessert. Especially delicious cut in half, topped with a little pure butter and lightly toasted. 10 minutes preparation, 25 min. baking.

HOT GOLDEN FRUIT COMPOTE

Maura Dillon Pichetto

1 lg. can peach halves (6 halves, heavy syrup)
1 lg. can apricot halves
1 med. can pineapple chunks
½ C. golden raisins

1 lg. banana - cut in half, then in quarters lengthwise
1 tsp. lemon juice
1 T. brown sugar
OPTIONAL: 2 T. dark rum

Lightly butter a 9×12" baking dish. Place in dish 6 peach halves (round side down). Place apricot half in each peach half. Place pineapple chunk in each apricot half. Put extra apricot halves, pineapple, raisins, and banana sections around peaches in dish. Pour in juice from peach can - should be about 1" around fruit. Add apricot juice if needed. Sprinkle lemon juice and sugar. Bake at 350° for 20 -30 minutes. Add dash of rum if desired. Serve plain or with vanilla ice cream or whipped cream.

NOTE: Can prepare in advance, bake while eating main course, and serve hot from oven. Good winter dessert. Serves 6.

GRAPE NUT PUDDING

Jean L. Artis and Dorothy Lockhart

4 or 5 eggs
1 can condensed milk
3 cans evaporated milk

2 tsp. pure lemon extract
1 tsp. vanilla extract
1 C. Post Grape Nuts with Raisins

In a large bowl beat eggs together. Stir in 1 can condensed milk with eggs and mix together. Add 3 cans evaporated milk. Add 2 tsp. lemon extract, 1 tsp. vanilla extract, and 1 cup Grape Nuts with Raisins. Stir all ingredients and pour into a deep circular baking pan ungreased. Just before placing in oven, drop in a very small chip of butter or margarine. Place in a preheated 350 - 400° oven (ovens may vary). Bake approximately 30 - 45 minutes until golden brown and a tester inserted in center comes out clean.

NOTE: Even if tester has small amount of pudding on it, the pudding can be removed from the oven and the custard will set. Enjoy!

STRAWBERRY JELLO MOLD

Diane Steinberg

1 (3-oz.) pkg. strawberry Jello
2 C. boiling water
1 C. cold water
1 C. sour cream

3 (10-oz.) pkgs. frozen sliced
strawberries, thawed in juice
1 sm. can crushed pineapple, drained
well

Dissolve Jello in boiling water and cold water, according to package directions. Stir in sour cream and beat with Jello until well blended. Add berries with juice and pineapple. Mix. Pour into a 12-cup mold. Refrigerate until firm.

OLD FASHIONED BREAD PUDDING

Gertrude E. Rodrigue

1 qt. milk
2 C. bread cubes
½ C. butter or margarine
2 eggs
⅓ C. sugar

½ tsp. salt
1 tsp. vanilla
few grains nutmeg
OPTIONAL: ½ C. raisins may be added
to mixture before baking

Scald milk, add bread cubes and butter or margarine. Beat eggs, add sugar and salt. Add milk mixture and vanilla extract. Pour into a baking dish. Sprinkle with nutmeg. Place in a pan of hot water. Bake in moderate (350°) oven 1 hour 15 minutes or until inserted knife comes out clean. Serves 4 to 6.

CHARLOTTE RUSSE

Francois Tanty - 1906

18 ladyfingers (or oblongs of sponge
cake)
1 circular slice of sponge cake
2 egg whites

¾ pt. heavy cream
1 T. powdered sugar
½ oz. gelatin, melted
1 tsp. vanilla

Take 18 ladyfingers (or oblongs of sponge cake 1×3×½"); brush edges with egg whites. Line the bottom of a plain round mold with some of the ladyfingers, placing cakes in the form of a star or rosette. Also stand cakes upright around the edge, placing so closely that the white of the egg will cement them. Place in 375° oven for 5 minutes to dry the egg. Whip ¾ pt. cream to stiff froth, add 1 T. powdered sugar, ½ oz. melted gelatin, and 1 tsp. vanilla. Beat thoroughly and pour into mold. Cover top with circular slice of sponge cake. Place on ice. When cold, turn upside down on dish, remove mold and serve.

CHOCOLATE MOUSSE

Adrianne Livadas

1½ C. water
3 tsp. inst. Sanka coffee
3 tsp. rum
1½ pkgs. Stella D'Oro
    Egg Jumble Cookies

1 lg. Cool Whip
sugar
3 tsp. Hershey chocolate powder
OPTIONAL: shaved white and dark
chocolate &/or nuts

In a bowl mix together water, coffee and rum. Soak cookies in this liquid mixture until cookies are wet but not mushy. Squeeze out excess liquid and line 8×11" pan with half the cookies. In another bowl mix together Cool Whip and chocolate powder, and sweeten to taste. Put half the Cool Whip mixture on top of the cookies and spread out evenly. Put remaining cookies (squeezed out and flattened) on top of Cool Whip mixture. Top with remaining Cool Whip mixture. Decorate with shaved white and dark chocolate or nuts.

NOTE: If not to be served immediately, mousse may be frozen. Thaw before serving.

EGGO WAFFLE DESSERT/SNACK

Margie Menendez

4 Eggo waffles - lightly toasted
1 ripe banana, sliced ¼" thick

1 C. strawberries, sliced
1 can Reddi Whip cream
chunks of cantaloupe (optional)

Place a layer of banana on the toasted waffles. Spread some cream over the bananas. Top all around with strawberries (and cantaloupe, if desired). Have fun and enjoy!

PECAN PIE

Veronica Stewart

2 C. water
½ lb. butter (2 sticks)
2 lbs. brown sugar
¼ C. Karo syrup

10 lg. eggs
1 T. cornstarch
1 lb. pecans
pie shell

Preheat oven to 400°. Bring to a boil water, butter, sugar and syrup. Mix together eggs and cornstarch. Slowly add boiled ingredients to egg mixture.

Place pie shell on large baking dish to catch drips. Line bottom of pie shell with pecans, then pour mixture carefully over pecans. Bake for 30 minutes.

CHOCOLATE TRUFFLES

Catherine Pellicano

16 oz. semisweet chocolate
1 C. heavy cream

½ C. chopped walnuts (or shredded coconut)

Break chocolate up into small pieces and place into a bowl. Over medium heat bring the heavy cream to a boil. Remove cream from burner and pour over the chocolate and let stand 5 - 10 minutes. Stir chocolate and cream mixture until smooth and set aside to cool for about 1 hour at room temperature. Once cooled, refrigerate the chocolate for 30 minutes and stir every 5 minutes. Take 1 level tsp. of chocolate and roll it in your palms until it is smooth and round. Roll the truffle in the chopped nuts or shredded coconut. Keep the truffles refrigerated until you are ready to serve them.

PEANUT BUTTER ICE CREAM PIE

Tina Walker

1½ C. graham cracker crumbs
⅓ C. butter, melted
¼ C. sugar
1 qt. vanilla ice cream, softened

1 C. peanut butter
½ pt. whipping cream, whipped
graham cracker crumbs
roasted peanuts, chopped for garnish

Combine 1½ C. cracker crumbs, butter and sugar. Press into 9" pie plate. Chill. Soften ice cream so that it can be stirred with a spoon. Stir peanut butter into ice cream. Fold whipped cream into mixture until well blended. Pour into the shell. If desired, sprinkle with more cracker crumbs and peanuts. Place in freezer to harden. If storing in freezer for more than a few hours, cover with freezer wrap.

RICE PUDDING

Francois Tanty - 1906

1 C. rice, boiled
4 eggs, beaten
1 C. sugar

1 C. raisins
1½ pts. milk
OPTIONAL: nutmeg

In large bowl, mix all ingredients. Put in ovenproof dish, bake at 350° until mixture is like custard and brown on top. If you like, sprinkle with nutmeg.

HAMANTASHEN

Helene Wayne

4 eggs
1 C. oil
1¼ C. sugar
2 tsp. vanilla

3 tsp. baking powder
½ tsp. salt
approximately 5½ C. flour
fillings of your choice (see below)

Beat eggs, mix in oil, sugar, vanilla, baking powder and salt. Add flour gradually, mix thoroughly. Knead till smooth enough to roll on floured board. Roll thin. Cut into 2 or 3" rounds. Add fillings: apricot or raspberry preserves, lekvar (prune) and/or moon (poppy seed). Draw up 3 sides and pinch together in form of a triangle. Place on a lightly greased baking sheet. Bake at 350° (in New York area), or at 325° (in Florida area) for about 15 - 30 minutes or until golden brown. Makes about 60.

FRUIT PUDDING

Francois Tanty - 1906

1 pint sugar
4 eggs, beaten
½ pint sour cream
½ tsp. baking soda

dash of salt
3 C. flour
1 qt. fruit (blackberries, blueberries, raspberries, etc.)

Mix the sugar with beaten eggs. Add the sour cream mixed with baking soda, a little salt, and the 3 cups of flour. Stir in all of the fruit and then place in a baking dish and bake. Serve hot, with any pudding sauce preferred.

STRAWBERRY-RHUBARB PIE

Mildred Nestor

1 C. sugar
3 T. flour
1 T. cornstarch
1 egg, well beaten
butter
OPTIONAL: sprinkle of salt

1 - 1½ C. fresh strawberries, cut into small slices (wild strawberries are excellent)
1 - 1½ C. rhubarb cut into small cubes
1 recipe plain pie crust mix or prepared pie crust

Mix sugar, flour and cornstarch together, add well beaten egg (and salt, if desired). Mix thoroughly. Line a 9 or 10" pie pan with the bottom crust; add in the filling. Add tiny pats of butter on top. Cover with the top crust. Bake in hot oven a few minutes to brown crust. Reduce the temperature to approximately 350°. Bake 35 minutes until done. May be served plain or with whipped cream.

PARTY PECAN TARTS

Selma Epstein

1 (8 oz.) pkg. cream cheese
2 C. sifted flour
1 box (1 lb.) light brown sugar
1½ C. chopped pecans
1 C. margarine

2 T. butter
3 eggs
½ tsp. vanilla
dash of salt

Let cream cheese and margarine soften to room temperature. Blend together with a fork. Add flour gradually. Blend with fork until well mixed. Press pastry into ungreased muffin pans, (1×1¾") to form a shell. Cream butter, brown sugar and eggs, salt and vanilla together until light and fluffy. Add pecans, mix thoroughly. Place 1 to 2 tsp. filling into each tart shell. Bake at 350° for 15 minutes. Lower temp. to 250° and bake for 10 minutes longer. Yields 60 to 72

BISCUIT RINGS

The Shatilar Family

1 lb. flour (10 biscuits)
¾ lb. sugar
2 lbs. butter or margarine

3 eggs
1 tsp. lemon juice

Combine and mix flour, sugar, butter, eggs and lemon juice. Make a flat sheet about ¼" thick. Use 2 cookie shapes (round - 1 lg, 1 sm.) to make rings. Preheat oven to 425 - 450°. Place on cookie sheet and bake until golden brown

MOM'S APPLESAUCE

Steve Schwartz

8 apples
¼ C. honey

¼ tsp. cinnamon
1½ C. water

Peel, core and quarter apples. Place them into a pan with all of the other ingredients. Cover and cook over medium heat for 15 - 20 minutes. Mash the apples with a potato masher or fork.

BANANA JAM

Ann Revi

8 ripe bananas, mashed well
3 lemons
3 C. sugar
3 C. water

Fresh green ginger root about size of
   walnut, cut into small pieces if
   desired
4 or 5 cloves

Squeeze juice from lemons and slice rind into paper-thin strips. Boil rind with water and sugar about 5 minutes. Add other ingredients. Cook slowly about ½ hour or more, stirring constantly to prevent scorching. It will be a yellow mush. Remove ginger root. Pour into sterilized jars and seal.

LIME MARMALADE

Ann Revi

6 - 10 limes
OPTIONAL: 1 - 2 lemons, juice only

water
sugar

This recipe takes three days to make.

FIRST DAY - Peel off outer green part of rind very thin, slice into paper-thin strips and save. Cut into small pieces or put through blender the rest of the limes - remove seeds. Measure rind and pulp, cover with 3 times as much water. Let soak overnight.

SECOND DAY - Boil mixture 15 minutes, let stand overnight.

THIRD DAY - Add juice of 1 or 2 lemons (if tart taste is desired). Measure fruit and equal amount of sugar. Bring to a boil, lower heat and let boil slowly ½ to 1 hour, until jelly stage is reached (slips off spoon). Skim foam. Let stand 1 hour. Stir. Fill sterilized jars and seal.

PEACH PRESERVES

Ann Revi

3 lbs. peaches (ripe)
1 orange
2 T. lemon juice

1 pkg. pectin (Sure-Jell)
5½ C. sugar
½ tsp. butter or margarine

Dip peaches in boiling water. Peel, pit and chop fine, or use potato masher. Peel, pit and cut up meat of orange. Add lemon juice. Measure 4½ C. prepared fruit. Place into large pot - stir in pectin. Bring to boil, add butter. Let boil, then add sugar. Stir well, let boil 1 minute or more. Remove from heat, skim off foam. Fill sterilized jars and seal.

BRONX MULBERRY JAM

Jacqueline Kutner

2 C. white or purple mulberries (a
mixture of both is ideal)

½ C. sugar
¼ C. water

Wash berries carefully and put them in a large saucepan with sugar and water. Mix, cover and simmer on low. Stir frequently till mixture is thick. Chill and serve. Tastes great on vanilla ice cream.

NOTE: Wild purple or white mulberries can really be found in The Bronx! In June, berries can be found in Van Cortlandt Park and along Riverdale Avenue and 254th Street.

RED PEPPER JAM

Ann Revi

5 or 6 lg. red peppers, seeded
4 C. sugar
1 C. apple cider vinegar

¼ C. lemon juice
2 pouches of Certo
½ tsp. margarine or butter to help
prevent foaming

Wash, seed and puree peppers to make 2 C. pulp. Add all ingredients together except Certo. Stir well, bring to a rapid boil and add Certo. Boil 1 minute. Remove from heat. Skim off foam. Fill sterilized jars, seal.

SOMETHING ELSE

Egg Cream
Iced Coffee
Irish Coffee
Horseradish
Candied Orange Peel
Fried Bananas
The Original Dave's Bronx Brunch
Corn Relish
Hollandaise Sauce
Eggs — Soft, Hard or Coddled
Eggs on the Raft
Scrambled Eggs
Yankee Stadium Hot Dog
Onion Relish or Dilled Onions
Refrigerator Pickles
Pumpkin Pickle
Pickled Watermelon Rind · Sweet Watermelon Pickle
Kennebunk Relish
Corn Pancakes
Blintze Souffle
Popcorn · Candied & Regular
Aunt Libby's Stuffing

EGG CREAM (secrets revealed, requires practice)

Robert Abrams

1½ oz. chocolate syrup   1 oz. of cold milk
5½ oz. seltzer (2 oz. pressurized)

[Editors' Note: Many people have asked, "What exactly is an Egg Cream, and why is it even called an Egg Cream?" Finally, we have an expert who can answer them. Robert Abrams, former Attorney General of the State of New York, former Borough President of The Bronx, formerly worked in his parents' luncheonette. One of their specialties was an Egg Cream! When he was asked how it got the name "Egg Cream," he applied simple Bronx logic, and answered, "Because it has no egg and it has no cream." He continued, "Its exotic-sounding name was probably created just to set it apart from mere chocolate sodas. 'Egg Creams' had charisma." Mr. Abrams reported that he recently paid $2.50 for an Egg Cream at a street fair.]

At 2000 Holland Avenue, in the Pelham Parkway area of The Bronx, the Abrams' luncheonette sold Egg Creams for 7¢ in the early 1950s. The price at Ben's Luncheonette gradually rose to 15¢ by the mid-1960s. Having made many thousands of them there, Ben's son, Bob, now reveals the secrets here for the first time in print:

Although the ingredients were widely known, the precise formula and specific technique to make this esoteric New York carbonated drink was closely held. Several nuances in its preparation made a significant difference in whether the Egg Cream had a full bodied flavor and majestic white foamy head, or was merely a mundane soda.

Made in an 8 oz. glass, two strong pushes on the chocolate syrup pump provided approximately 1½ ounces. Tipping the glass at a 30° angle under the seltzer spout, you slowly injected about 3½ ounces. At that point you poured in about 1 ounce of cold milk.

Now you were at the critical juncture which most practitioners did not appreciate. You gave a sudden spurt of seltzer (pressurized) into the glass, which produced foam. Then you placed a 12" stainless steel spoon into the glass, above the soda line, to slow the flow as you pumped additional seltzer into the glass. As it hit the spoon it sprayed against the inside of the glass, whereupon you rapidly stirred the ingredients. With a strong enough wrist movement to stir up the syrup at the bottom of the glass, and off the sides, you obtained a vigorous and thorough shaking of this carbonated concoction.

(continued)

EGG CREAM (Continued)

The wonderful white head of foam began to tower at the top of this brew. By the time the glass was placed on the counter for the customer's consumption there was a white foam head about ½" in the glass with ¼" more rising above and beyond the rim of the glass. If the person behind the counter was unskilled, or unsophisticated, the foam in the Egg Cream would take up one-third of the glass, producing an unsatisfactory drink and/or there would be a weak little frizzly head.

One of the tragedies of modern times is that the Egg Cream is hard to find in The Bronx, or for that matter, anywhere in New York City. Its demise has sorely impacted on the character of native New Yorkers. If made right, when the Egg Cream is placed on the counter, the customer will behold the stately appearance of the drink and will be transformed to a mood of total contentment as it is consumed. Egg Cream mavens drank directly from the glass. Some people requested a straw, which would be provided, along with a stifled snicker.

ICED COFFEE

Isabelle Lee Hermalyn

coffee
sugar

milk
ice cubes

Make a pot of coffee. Put sugar and milk into coffee while it is boiling hot. Let it cool and then pour the coffee into tumblers filled with ice cubes.

IRISH COFFEE

Somchai Likiprakong

1 jigger Irish Whiskey
1 to 2 tsp. sugar

strong coffee
whipped cream

Make coffee. Place whiskey into mug; add sugar and stir to dissolve. Fill mug with hot coffee, top with whipped cream.

HORSERADISH

Francois Tanty · 1906

2 or 3 horseradish roots, grated
salt and pepper

8 oz. vinegar

In a bowl, thoroughly mix spices and horseradish. Pour vinegar over the mixture.

CANDIED ORANGE PEEL

Ann Revi

orange peel (small plastic bag full) cold water
sugar

Wash orange peels twice, then break up peels into 4" pieces. Cover with cold water. Bring to a boil but do not boil. Drain water off. Repeat process 2 more times. Measure or weigh softened peel - add same amount of sugar. Cover with water, stir, bring to boil, then let simmer, stirring often until all syrup is gone. Be careful not to burn peel at this point. Empty onto a buttered pan and spread on pan; let cool, work with fork to loosen.

Water may be saved to add to iced tea. Whole process takes about 3 hours. Use heavy weight aluminum pot. Store in closed can when cold.

FRIED BANANAS

Charles Vogeler Company - c.1880s

12 med. bananas   ½ C. milk
oil for frying   4 T. flour
BATTER: dash of salt
2 eggs

Pare a dozen bananas and cut each lengthwise into three slices. Make batter by combining the eggs, milk, flour and salt. Dip the banana slices into the batter and deep-fry until golden brown.

THE ORIGINAL DAVE'S BRONX BRUNCH

David Meth

fresh hot assorted bagels -   Bermuda onion or sweet Spanish
preferably not plain   onion
excellent cream cheese   ripe beefsteak tomatoes
thinly sliced Nova Scotia salmon -   capers
   tasted at store first

Go out Sunday morning and buy all ingredients before brunch. Slice bagels sandwich style. Add a schmear of cream cheese. Delicately place thin slices of Nova on top. Cut medium slices of tomato and onion. Place liberal amount of capers on the top of onions and tomato. Add the top half of the bagel and sink your teeth into a delectable treat, to properly start your Sunday.

CORN RELISH

Ann Revi

12 - 15 ears of corn (2 qts. kernels)	2 T. salt
2 C. chopped sweet red peppers	2 tsp. celery seed
2 C. chopped sweet green peppers	2 T. hot mustard
4 C. celery	1 tsp. turmeric
1 C. onion	¼ C. white flour
½ - ¾ C. honey	OPTIONAL: ½ sm. cabbage
1 qt. vinegar	

Using stainless steel or enameled pot, cook corn on the cob 3 minutes. Dip into cold water, drain. Cut kernels from cob. Combine all vegetables, except corn, with honey, vinegar, salt and celery seed. Simmer 15 minutes. Mix mustard, turmeric, flour with ½ C. water. Add it along with the corn to other ingredients. Simmer 5 minutes, stirring constantly. If desired add more honey for sweeter taste. Pack to within ½" of top, into sterilized canning jars, seal. Process for 10 minutes in boiling water bath. Cool before storing. Makes about 8 pints.

HOLLANDAISE SAUCE

June Bingham

2 egg yolks (lg. or extra lg.)	4 T. butter or margarine
4 T. cream	juice of one lemon (med. size)

Mix the yolks, cream and butter in an ordinary saucepan. Just before heating it, add lemon juice. Stir constantly. It thickens within a minute. Serve immediately.

EGGS — SOFT, HARD OR CODDLED

M. Lampell

2 eggs

Place 2 eggs into a pan of cold water over medium heat. Once water boils, reduce heat and allow to simmer for:
Soft cooked - 2 - 3 minutes. Hard cooked - 10 - 15 minutes, then...
remove from heat, place into cold water to cease any further cooking. Crack shell and roll egg between your palms to make removing shell an easy task.

To coddle, put into boiling water, cover, remove from heat for 6 - 8 minutes.

NOTE: To tell if that single egg in your refrigerator is hard-boiled, simply spin it on its pointed end. Hard-boiled eggs will spin, all other eggs will not.

EGGS ON THE RAFT

Sol Montcalm Hermalyn

2 eggs
1 slice of bread

butter or light oil (Canola oil)

Melt butter or light oil in a fry pan over medium to medium high flame. Place bread with a hole poked out of its center into pan. Place 2 whole eggs onto the bread. Carefully push the yolks to the center and make sure that the egg whites soak into the entire bread. Cover the pan. When the yolk starts firming, turn over entire bread and cook until the yolk is the consistency you wish.

SCRAMBLED EGGS

Charles Vogeler Company - c.1880s

8 to 10 eggs
1 T. butter
4 oz. milk
salt and pepper

1 T. minced parsley
toast (crustless)
hot milk, salted peppered and buttered

Combine butter, milk, salt, pepper, and parsley in a frying pan. When the mixture boils, stir into it 8 or 10 eggs. Beat and stir until they are well mixed and cease to run over the pan. Line a dish with crustless toast dipped in hot milk, salted, peppered, and buttered - pour the eggs on this bed.

YANKEE STADIUM HOT DOG

Anonymous

1 Ball Park Hot Dog
1 Hot Dog roll

OPTIONAL: mustard, sauerkraut, relish
and a cold drink

Preferably eaten at the stadium during a hot July day game when the Yankees are playing the Red Sox, and winning!

ONION RELISH OR DILLED ONIONS

Dolores Lessner

6 white onions
½ C. sugar
2 tsp. salt

¾ C. dill seed
½ C. white vinegar
¼ C. water

Slice onions into thin rings, place in a bowl. Combine remaining ingredients in a saucepan and slowly bring to a rolling boil. Remove from heat, pour over onions. Let stand until cool. Store in refrigerator.

REFRIGERATOR PICKLES

Anna May Mann

4 C. sugar
4 C. cider vinegar
½ C. salt
1 tsp. turmeric

1 tsp. celery seed
1 tsp. mustard seed
3 - 4 cucumbers
1 - 2 onions sliced thin

Mix together sugar, vinegar and spices till syrupy. Do not heat. Wash and sterilize 4 pint jars. Slice onions and cucumbers to fill jars. Stir syrup well, pour over cucumbers and onions in jars. Screw on lids. Refrigerate at least 5 days before using. Will keep in refrigerator for at least 9 months.

PUMPKIN PICKLE

Ann Revi

5 lb. pumpkin
1 tsp. whole cloves
2 whole allspice
1 T. broken cinnamon stick

1 - 1½ qt. white vinegar
9 C. sugar
cheesecloth
canning jars

Wash, pare, trim and cut pumpkin into 1" cubes. Tie spices in cheesecloth. Put vinegar, sugar and spices (cloves, allspice, cinnamon) into an enameled pot and heat to boiling. Add pumpkin - (it will shrink as it cooks down) and cook in syrup until tender (about ½ hour - do not overcook). Pack in sterile jars to ½" from top. Seal the jars. Process in boiling water bath 10 minutes, remove. Cool before storing. About 4 qts. Flavor and taste is similar to watermelon pickle.

PICKLED WATERMELON RIND - SWEET WATERMELON PICKLE

Ann Revi

2 lbs. watermelon rind (from
    one melon)
2½ qts. water
½ C. salt
green food color - a few drops
2 C. vinegar

1 lemon, sliced thin
4 C. sugar
1 tsp. whole cloves
½ tsp. whole allspice
1 stick whole cinnamon

Peel and trim rind. Cut into 1" pieces. Soak overnight in salt solution: 2 qts. water and ½ cup salt. Drain off salted water, rinse with fresh, then cover with fresh water and boil till tender. In an enameled pot combine remaining ingredients with 2 cups of water. Boil 5 minutes, then add rind. Simmer until clear, add green food color. Fill sterilized jars and seal. Process in hot water bath for 5 minutes. Remove and cool before storing.

KENNEBUNK RELISH

Ann Revi

2 sweet red peppers
2 sweet green peppers
2 lbs. fresh green tomatoes
2 lbs. fresh red tomatoes
1 sm. head of cabbage
¾ qt. onions
1 bunch celery

6 T. coarse salt plain (un-iodized)
1 qt. white cider vinegar
1 C. (or more) brown sugar
1 stick whole cinnamon
1 tsp. whole cloves
1 tsp. dry mustard

Wash, trim, hand chop all vegetables, coarsely. Place into plastic container. Sprinkle with salt. Let stand overnight. In an enameled or stainless steel pot, place the vinegar, sugar and spices (tied in a cloth bag). Bring to boil, simmer. Drain vegetables, squeeze out as much liquid as possible. Add to vinegar solution. Cook until clear. Taste for desired sweetness. Fill sterilized jars and seal. Process in hot water bath for 10 minutes. Remove from pot. Let stand until cold. Store in cold place.

CORN PANCAKES

Francois Tanty - 1906

2 tsp. baking powder
1 pt. cornmeal
½ pt. flour

dash of salt
2 eggs, beaten
milk, enough to make a batter

Make batter by combining all of the above ingredients. Pour batter on a hot greased frying pan and remove when golden brown on both sides.

BLINTZE SOUFFLE

Ronnie Greenberg

12 frozen blintzes
4 eggs
¼ tsp. salt
½ C. orange juice

1½ C. sour cream
1 stick butter
½ C. sugar
1 tsp. vanilla

Butter casserole and place in blintzes. Mix all ingredients together. Pour over blintzes. Bake 1 hour at 375°, or until golden brown.

POPCORN - CANDIED & REGULAR

Big Ed Lukawski

½ C. kernels for popcorn
1 tsp. vegetable oil
grated cheese
2 T melted butter
salt and pepper

CARAMEL SYRUP (for Candied
   Popcorn)
1½ T. butter
1½ C. brown sugar
6 T. water

REGULAR: Cook over high heat in heavy skillet, covered with a lid. Keep pan moving at all times. When corn stops popping, remove uncooked kernels. Add salt, pepper, grated cheese and melted butter (2 T.).

CANDIED: First make plain popcorn, remove uncooked kernels. Make the CARAMEL SYRUP: In a pot stir the three ingredients until the sugar is dissolved, bring to a boil. Cover and cook for 3 minutes or so. Uncover and cook until mixture reaches a soft stage. Then pour over plain popcorn, stirring gently with a wooden spoon until well-coated.

AUNT LIBBY'S STUFFING

Libby Parisse

1 C. onions
1 C. celery, chopped
1 lb. sausage meat, removed from casing

1 (12 oz.) pkg. Pepperidge Farm
   herb-seasoned bread cubes
1 C. soft breadcrumbs
OPTIONAL: bouillon cube

Saute onions and celery together with the sausage meat. Add to the other ingredients. Mix well - stuff turkey or place in baking pan and bake. If more moisture is needed, add a bouillon cube, dissolved in a cup of hot water.

The Bronx County Historical Society is supported in part with public funds and services provided through
The Department of Cultural Affairs and
The Department of Parks and Recreation of the City of New York,
The City Council Delegation of The Bronx,
The Office of the Bronx Borough President,
The Bronx Delegations of The NYS Assembly and The NYS Senate,
The New York State Council on the Arts,
The New York State Office of Parks, Recreation and Historic Preservation,
The State Library and the New York State Archives and Records Administration.

BOOKS FROM THE
BRONX COUNTY HISTORICAL SOCIETY

1. **The Bronx It Was Only Yesterday: 1935-1965.** (Ultan & Hermalyn)
   (NEW) A glorious photo montage of The Bronx during this era
   of growth and stability..

2. **The Beautiful Bronx: 1920-1950.** (Ultan)
   A treasure chest of memories of the exciting years of The Bronx.....

3. **The Bronx in the Innocent Years: 1890-1925.** (Ultan & Hermalyn)
   Colorful first-person reminiscences and rare historical
   photographs provide a nostalgic glimpse into the past.....................

4. **History in Asphalt: The Origin of Bronx Street
   & Place Names.** (McNamara)   (Third Edition)
   Did you ever wonder how your street got its name? This fascinating
   560 page encyclopedia describes the history of Bronx names ....

5. **The Bronx in Print: An Annotated Catalogue of
   Books and Pamphlets About The Bronx.** (Kuhta & Rodriguez)
   A handy guide for researchers..

6. **Elected Public Officials of The Bronx Since 1898.** (Tosi & Hermalyn)
   (NEW) A compilation of ten Bronx offices, the names of the officials,
   their party affiliations and years of service. This is the only
   work of its kind in New York City ....(Fourth Edition)

7. **History of Morris Park Racecourse.** (DiBrino)
   An illustrated history of the famous Bronx racecourse
   and the Morris Family..

8. **Poems of Edgar Allan Poe at Fordham.** (Beirne)
   A collection of Poe's works while he lived in his Fordham Cottage ..

9. **Legacy of the Revolution.** (Ultan)
   A history of the landmark Valentine-Varian
   House, one of the City's oldest structures.......................................

10. **The Bronx Triangle: A Portrait of Norwood.** (Mead)
    An illustrated history of this northern Bronx neighborhood...........

11. **Genealogy of The Bronx.** (Hermalyn & Tosi)
    An annotated guide to sources of information................................

12. **Theatres of The Bronx.** (Miller)
    Photographs of the famous movie theatres of The Bronx ....

13. **Latin Bicentennial.** (Serrano)
    This Spanish and English comic book discusses the Hispanic
    peoples of The Bronx ....

14. **McNamara's Old Bronx.** (McNamara)
   John McNamara's incomparable articles from his "Bronx in History" column in *The Bronx Press Review* spans the centuries with stories of the people of The Bronx..

15. **The Bronx in The Frontier Era: From The Beginning to 1696.** (Ultan)
   The first comprehensive volume in The Society's new series on *The History of The Bronx* ....

16. **West Farms Local History Curriculum Guide.** (Hopkins)
   Suggested objectives, lessons, activities, and resources for all grades ....

17. **Landmarks of The Bronx.** (Hermalyn & Kornfeld)
   Comprehensive list of designated and proposed landmarks of The Bronx; description of the landmark law and its process ....**Revised Edition**

18. **The South Bronx and the Founding of America.** (Garrison)
   This activity book for teachers and students provides a concise historical account of the early settling of The Bronx......................

19. **Morris High School and the Creation of the New York City Public High School System.** (Hermalyn)
   (**NEW**) This is the story of the extraordinary educational reforms of the 1890s which peaked with the opening of Morris High in 1897 ....

20. **Edgar Allan Poe at Fordham.** (McAuley)
   A teacher's guide and workbook on the life of this great writer........

21. **The Signers of the Constitution of the United States.** (Quinn)
   Sprightly character sketches with original drawings of the Signers including The Bronx's own Gouverneur Morris...............................

22. **The Signers of the Declaration of Independence.** (Quinn)
   Interesting character sketches and original drawings of the Signers of the Declaration including The Bronx's Lewis Morris ....

23. **Presidents of the United States.** (Ultan)
   Absorbing character outlines of the men who have held the office; essays on the origins of the Presidency and the electoral college.....

24. **Chief Justices of The U.S. Supreme Court.** (Lankevich)
   (**NEW**) The story of the men who have been the Chief Justices of the U.S. Supreme Court..

25. **The First House of Representatives and The Bill of Rights.** (Lankevich)
   (**NEW**) The story behind the Bill of Rights and the men who established the first House of Representatives ....

26. **The First Senate of The United States.** (Streb)
   (**NEW**) Explores the key figures in the upper house of the Congress in 1789 ......

27. New York City at the Turn of the Century (Beirne)

(NEW) A captivating collection of essays on New York City with 42
original paintings in full color ....

28. 350th Anniversary of The Bronx Commemorative Issue.
This work celebrates The Bronx with essays on Jonas Bronck,
transportation and The Bronx at the turn of the 20th century...............

29. Bicentennial of the United States Constitution Commemorative Issue.
This special edition features articles on Gouverneur Morris, the
Penman of the Constitution and a description of colonial money ....

30. 25 Year Index to The Bronx County Historical Society Journal.
This comprehensive index includes thousands of references to
local events, individuals, institutions, schools and businesses.
An invaluable research tool for New York history and genealogy...........

31. Local History Classroom Resource Guide
(NEW) Suggested activities, lessons and charts for all grades ....

GIFTS IN THE HISTORIC TRADITION

A.   **THE BRONX AFGHAN**   **$50.00**

(NEW) 50" x 65" 100% cotton. Depicts scenes of Bronx institutions: The Zoo,
Wave Hill, Historic Houses, Botanical Garden and Yankee Stadium.

B. THE GRAND CONCOURSE PRINT **$20.00 per print** **$110.00 framed**
A top quality print of the 1892 proposed plan for the Concourse. It depicts the
entire west Bronx and upper Manhattan printed on 25" x 12" acid free stock.

C. *(a.)* **TILES OF THE VALENTINE-VARIAN HOUSE**   **$10.00**
     (b.) **AND THE EDGAR ALLAN POE COTTAGE**   **tile**
Each historic house is represented by a charming line drawing on a white ceramic
tile. They are decorative, useful and commemorate beloved Bronx landmarks.

D.   **HISTORIC SCENES OF THE BRONX:**   **$32.00**
      SET OF SIX OLD FASHIONED GLASSES   **set**
These unique glasses are each decorated with designs of historic sites.

When ordering books and gifts, please make your check payable to:
The Bronx County Historical Society
3309 Bainbridge Ave., The Bronx, NY 10467
Telephone: (718) 881-8900

If ordering in N.Y. C., include New York City Sales Tax (8¼%)

Shipping and handling for first item $4.00, $2.00 per each additional item to one address.

Prices subject to change.
For a complete list of videotapes and radio show cassettes, contact the office.

THE BRONX COUNTY
HISTORICAL SOCIETY

The Bronx County Historical Society was founded in 1955 for the purpose of promoting knowledge, interest and research in The Bronx. The Society administers The Museum of Bronx History, Edgar Allan Poe Cottage, a Research Library, and The Bronx County Archives; publishes books, journals and newsletters; conducts school programs, historical tours, lectures, courses, archaeological digs and commemorations; designs exhibitions, sponsors various expeditions, and produces the *Out Of The Past* radio show and cable television programs. The Society is active in furthering the arts, in preserving the natural resources of The Bronx, and in creating a sense of pride in the Bronx community.

Members of The Bronx County Historical Society receive:

A subscription to

The Bronx County Historical Society Journal
published semi-annually

The Bronx Historian Newsletter

Free admission to

MUSEUM OF BRONX HISTORY
3266 Bainbridge Avenue at East 208th Street
The Bronx, New York

EDGAR ALLAN POE COTTAGE
Kingsbridge Road and Grand Concourse
The Bronx, New York

Invitation to

The Society's Annual High School
Valedictorians Awards Program,
Historical Tours, Lectures, Exhibitions
and other Educational Projects

To join, please write or telephone:
THE BRONX COUNTY HISTORICAL SOCIETY
3309 Bainbridge Avenue, The Bronx, New York 10467
Telephone: (718) 881-8900

*Administered by The Bronx County Historical Society
by agreement with The NYC Department of Cultural Affairs*

**Offices, Research Library and Archives of
The Bronx County Historical Society
3309 Bainbridge Ave.
The Bronx NY 10467**

(718) 881-8900

The Bronx County Historical Society Research Library and Archives

The New Home of

THE BRONX COUNTY ARCHIVES

3313 BAINBRIDGE AVENUE

The Bronx County Historical Society has earned a national reputation for preserving the heritage of the people of The Bronx. Renowned for its Research Library and its collection of historical information on The Bronx, including books, publications, reports, pamphlets, photographs, drawings, and charts, the Society saw its historical collection grow considerably when in 1974 it assumed responsibility for an additional million items which were then established as The Bronx Archives.

The Archives contain original documents, manuscripts, record books, maps and city directories going back to 1698. This collection is a prime source of information on the economic, social and political history of The Bronx as well as of New York City and Westchester County.

VALENTINE-VARIAN HOUSE

c. 1758

MUSEUM OF BRONX HISTORY

*The Valentine-Varian House is owned and administered by
The Bronx County Historical Society.*

Saturday 10:00 A.M.-4:00 P.M., Sunday 1:00 P.M.-5:00 P.M.
Open Monday to Friday 9:00 A.M.-5:00 P.M.
for Guided Tours by appointment

Bainbridge Avenue at East 208th Street
The Bronx, New York 10467
Telephone: (718) 881-8900

❖ ❖ ❖

Mr. William F. Beller purchased the Valentine-Varian House in 1905. His son, Mr. William C. Beller, donated the landmark structure to The Bronx County Historical Society in 1965. In recognition of this, the trustees in 1974 established The Society's most prestigious annual award, the William Beller Award of Excellence and Achievement.

THE EDGAR ALLAN POE COTTAGE

The Grand Concourse & East Kingsbridge Road
The Bronx, New York
HOURS:
Saturday: 10:00 a.m. - 4:00 p.m.
Sunday: 1:00 p.m. - 5:00 p.m.
Group Tours Weekdays by Appointment Only
$2.00 Admission Per Person
Main Office (718) 881-8900

Administered by
The Bronx County Historical Society
in agreement with the
New York City Department of
Parks & Recreation

The Bronx County Historical Society Research Library and Archives

HOW TO ORDER
THE BRONX COOKBOOK

To order additional copies of **The Bronx Cookbook**, fill in and return an order form with your check or moneyorder to:

The Bronx County Historical Society
Cookbook Project
3309 Bainbridge Ave.
The Bronx NY 10467

(718) 881-8900

The Bronx Cookbook is $12.00 per copy, while supplies last.
          Price is subject to change.
Shipping & Handling per copy is $2.00, for a total of $14.00 each.
NYC Sales tax is 8¼. New York City residents please add $1.00 for
          a total of $15.00 per copy.
Please send me _____ copies. I have enclosed $_____
Please make check or money order payable to **The Bronx Historical Society.**
Please do NOT send cash.

YOUR NAME:_____

ADDRESS _____

CITY_____STATE_____ZIP_____

. . . .

The Bronx Cookbook is $12.00 per copy, while supplies last.
          Price is subject to change.
Shipping & Handling per copy is $2.00, for a total of $14.00 each.
NYC Sales tax is 8¼. New York City residents please add $1.00 for
          a total of $15.00 per copy.
Please send me _____ copies. I have enclosed $_____
Please make check or money order payable to **The Bronx Historical Society.**
Please do NOT send cash.

YOUR NAME:_____

ADDRESS _____

CITY_____STATE_____ZIP_____

RECIPE COLLECTION SHEET

Please Type or Print Only One Recipe On This Form.
If you need more space, use the back, or another paper.

Circle category, as used in this cookbook:

APPETIZERS
SOUPS & SANDWICHES
SALADS & VEGETABLES
BREADS & ROLLS

MAIN DISHES
MEAT, POULTRY, SEAFOOD
CAKES & COOKIES, JAMS & PRESERVES, DESSERTS
SOMETHING ELSE

RECIPE TITLE: _____

YOUR NAME: _____

PHONE (Only in case we have a question) _____

INGREDIENTS: Standard Abbreviations used in this cookbook
C. = Cup T. = Tablespoon tsp. = teaspoon pt. = pint qt. = quart oz. = ounce
lb(s). = pound(s) pkg. = package sm. = small med. = medium lg. = large

_____

_____

_____

_____

_____

DIRECTIONS _____

_____

_____

_____

_____

_____

_____

_____

Please send to:
The Bronx County Historical Society
Cookbook Project
3309 Bainbridge Ave.
The Bronx NY 10467

(718) 881-8900

RECIPE COLLECTION SHEET
Please Type or Print Only One Recipe On This Form.
If you need more space, use the back, or another paper.

Circle category, as used in this cookbook:

APPETIZERS
SOUPS & SANDWICHES
SALADS & VEGETABLES
BREADS & ROLLS

MAIN DISHES
MEAT, POULTRY, SEAFOOD
CAKES & COOKIES, JAMS & PRESERVES, DESSERTS
SOMETHING ELSE

RECIPE TITLE:_____

YOUR NAME:_____

PHONE (Only in case we have a question)_____

INGREDIENTS: Standard Abbreviations used in this cookbook
C.= Cup T.= Tablespoon tsp.= teaspoon pt. = pint qt. = quart oz. = ounce
lb(s).= pound(s) pkg. = package sm. = small med. = medium lg. = large

_____

_____

_____

_____

_____

DIRECTIONS_____

_____

_____

_____

_____

_____

_____

Please send to:
The Bronx County Historical Society
Cookbook Project
3309 Bainbridge Ave.
The Bronx NY 10467

(718) 881-8900

RECIPE COLLECTION SHEET
Please Type or Print Only One Recipe On This Form.
If you need more space, use the back, or another paper.

Circle category, as used in this cookbook:

APPETIZERS

SOUPS & SANDWICHES

SALADS & VEGETABLES

BREADS & ROLLS

MAIN DISHES

MEAT, POULTRY, SEAFOOD

CAKES & COOKIES, JAMS & PRESERVES, DESSERTS

SOMETHING ELSE

RECIPE TITLE:_____

YOUR NAME:_____

PHONE (Only in case we have a question)_____

INGREDIENTS: Standard Abbreviations used in this cookbook

C.= Cup T.= Tablespoon tsp.= teaspoon pt. = pint qt. = quart oz. = ounce
lb(s).= pound(s) pkg. = package sm. = small med. = medium lg. = large

_____

_____

_____

_____

_____

DIRECTIONS_____

_____

_____

_____

_____

_____

_____

Please send to:
The Bronx County Historical Society
Cookbook Project
3309 Bainbridge Ave.
The Bronx NY 10467

(718) 881-8900

Waldorf Cafeteria, 140 East 170th Street, 1950s. For decades, there were cafeterias on most of the major shopping streets in The Bronx, many of which served as centers of long political debates over a single cup of coffee.

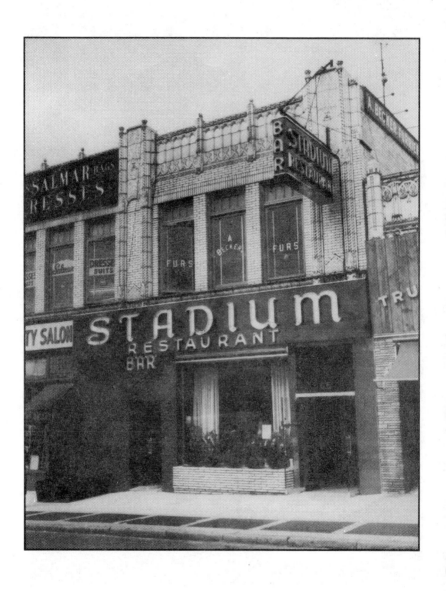

Stadium Restaurant, 65 East 161st Street, 1950s. The area around Yankee Stadium has always had restaurants that cater to baseball fans as well as the local community.

The Bronx County Historical Society Research Library and Archives